A Call to Joy

Celebrating the God

of Unconditional Love

No part of this book may be reproduced or transmitted in any form or by any means, electronic or mechanical, including photocopy, recording, or by any informational storage and retrieval, without the written permission of the publisher, except where permitted by law.

© 2018

All rights reserved.

Edited By: Edit This One, LLC., Fairfax, IA
www.editTHISone.com

Published By: Edit This One, LLC d/b/a Wordy Gerty Publishing

Wordy Gerty Publishing

Cover created by: Steven F. Deslippe using a photo provided by Terry Lindsley.

ISBN 978-0-9981046-6-9

A Call To Joy is a timely and refreshing reflection on God and religion. A journey from antiquated teachings on God and religion to faith, love and soul growth.
---Monica Ferreira – Salt Lake City, UT

A Call To Joy is a book that calls the seeking soul to a deeper level of intimacy with the Holy One that is in us and ever present with us. It is a call to an authentic relationship with Unconditional Love, rather than an external faith of rule following and unexplored theological dogma.
---Rev. Dorothy Lawson, BCC-Supervisor of Pastoral Care CHI Health-Metro Omaha/Council Bluffs

I grew up and was married in the Catholic Church. Unfortunately, my marriage only lasted just over a year. Once I was separated, I had a hard time going back to the Catholic Church. I have been fighting with this for many years and now that I have read this book, I feel better about not attending any type of congregation. I do believe that there is a God, but I also believe that we can pray anywhere and we will be heard. Many times I pray to my parents for guidance, I feel that they are my Guardian Angels. I also believe that I connected with Terry (and Barb) for this very reason. It was time for me to figure it out. Thank you so much Terry for your help and for writing this book.
---Tina Rosekrans, Edit This One, LLC – Fairfax, IA

Dedication

This work is dedicated to
those souls who have the courage
to explore the challenge that
has been given to us –
to discover for ourselves
what is the meaning of love.

Table of Contents

Preface i

Introduction iv

Author's Note viii

Chapter 1 – The Problem of Beliefs 1

Chapter 2 – About God 14

Chapter 3 – About Jesus and All of Us 27

Chapter 4 – People of the Book 37

Chapter 5 – Developing a Good Crap Detector 52

Chapter 6 – Psychology of the Soul 67

Chapter 7 – Do we need Organized Religion? 81

Chapter 8 – Prayer 97

Chapter 9 – Living well – Dying well 114

Chapter 10 – Charting Your Own Course 124

Afterword

Acknowledgments

Appendix

Preface

This book may or may not be for you. After reading the following, you'll know if you are ready for it.

- If you sense a spiritual void in your life and are looking for answers, this is a guide to a more vibrant spirituality.
- If following the rules of religion is dragging you down, relax because there is a better way to live.
- If you like the church you belong to, but find Sunday services and sermons preached lacking meaning, this may help you to enrich that experience.
- If you question certain beliefs of your church or upbringing, then read on.
- If you are willing to re-examine your beliefs in light of new understandings, insights and knowledge, this guide will help.
- If you have the courage to look at and discard some old beliefs that no longer serve you, read on.
- If you are totally fed up with organized religion, don't give up! You can live a full spiritual life without it. Trust yourself and God to develop a dynamic and meaningful spirituality that animates everything you do and you'll love it.

- If you feel religion places burdens, demands and obligates you, that you would rather be free of, stay tuned.
- If you are fearful of Satan and the prospect of hell, there is good news.
- If your concept of god includes judgment, vengeance, and punishment, then by all means read on. This god doesn't exist.
- If you were told that your religion provided the only way to heaven after this lifetime, this is not true. There are many paths to God.
- If you think that you have only one lifetime to live and that you will be judged when you die, you'll be relieved to learn otherwise.
- If the thought of being in the presence of god makes you fearful and uneasy, you severely misunderstand your Creator, and good news awaits.
- If you have trouble with some of the concepts outlined in the Bible, there is much here that will help you understand what that book is all about.
- If you want to know what God has revealed throughout the ages and very recently, you'll be pleasantly surprised.
- If you want to stay as a member of a congregation, but want to make some changes, this is possible.

- If you are not currently a member of a church, this book will not say you should belong to a church.

This is a guide for those who want to understand who they really are and why they are here in this lifetime; to understand their role and place in the larger context of God and the universe. You can finally relax with a comfortable spirituality that is free of fear and retribution. This work will speak to those who do or don't belong to a church.

Introduction

This was a project begun while I was undergoing chemotherapy treatments for non-Hodgkin's lymphoma cancer. I needed something to keep my mind active and life interesting. While I was writing it seemed that I had a lot to share, but with whom? I was not sure who was my intended audience. I thought perhaps it was more of a personal exercise to journal my thoughts on an evolving spirituality, namely mine, but I also thought there might be others who could benefit from sharing these ideas.

An Old Jewish saying states there are three things we should do that will outlast us and be our legacy. These are plant a tree, have a child and write a book. I have planted trees, and I have a family and now this work.

Over the years, I have benefitted from books that resonated with me. These seemed to awaken in me new levels of awareness. What others had to say inspired me to rethink my beliefs and values. I have never lost my interest in questioning everything. I love living with life's questions especially when it comes to sensible spiritual beliefs. Because of this and my spiritual journey through the seminary education, Catholic priesthood and eventually to marriage, I have some valued experience from which to draw.

I consider myself sort of a spiritual maverick. In my work as hospital chaplain, people often ask me if I belong to any church. I have learned to answer by saying that my background is Catholic, that I am now retired and, at this time, do not belong to any faith community. I had to dance around this issue when asked for a bio to be included in a chaplain directory for the hospital, but I am comfortable with my current status. I feel accepted by the hospital staff. Patient and staff feedback appears to be positive and I find the hospital ministry personally meaningful.

I have never received any paperwork from the Diocese or Rome saying that I was no longer a priest, but I know that I do not have the blessing of the Catholic Church to administer any of the sacraments, nor do I feel the need to challenge that assumption. Besides, being a hospital chaplain, I have to respect the faiths of everyone I work with and I prefer not be tied to one sect or faith tradition.

If there's one theme that is consistent throughout this work, it is that unless we take a serious look at what we believe, we'll be stuck with some outdated beliefs that can blind us in searching for meaning. All organized religions are being challenged. The old spirituality does not speak to many anymore. A lot of that has to do with a person's concept of God. A new spirituality is emerging. I am excited about it and want others to know about it. It is what's happening now and it is the work of the Holy Spirit. These are very special times we live in and I might add, critical times for humanity and the planet as well. No other generation has had to face the overpowering issues we face today. Mankind needs to open its eyes to what is going on. So it is important that we not continue on with business as usual, but open our eyes to what is happening in our world and not get stuck in a belief system that blinds us to it all. God is speaking to us today. We need to listen up.

If you find something interesting in this work, then it will have benefitted someone besides me. I believe the Holy Spirit works with everyone in unique ways, but always for our highest good. May you be able to listen to the Spirit's guidance in your life and in so doing, touch the lives of many others in a meaningful and loving way.

The Lord of the Dance: The Good News should be the message that all spiritual seekers rejoice in sharing. It is difficult to engage people in a conversation about God and how he/she is active in our lives and in the world. When many think of god, they don't want to dance or feel joyful. Right away, people see in their mind's eye, an image that is less than appealing. They don't even want to be friends with the Divine. Some have discarded a hostile, punishing and jealous god, but don't have a better concept or experience that they can believe in.

Many sacred texts clearly portray a god who has a lot of conditions attached to whether god will love us or not. As a result over the centuries we have the "chosen people," the "saved and the damned," the "in group" and the "outcasts," the "true religion" and all other false notions. Add to these: "sin," "hell," and the "devil," "heresy," the need for "redemption," "baptism," "soldiers for Christ," the need to "convert" the pagans or infidels so they can be saved, and the "Last Judgment."

All of this reflects how the original message of Jesus and other spiritual masters became distorted and the baggage that the original concept has accumulated over time. The Bible, and many other "sacred texts" are tainted with the additions of those who authored the texts. They contain messages and even threats issued in the name of god... "do this or else," or "god will love us only if we follow his commandments." These do not portray a God who loves all of his/her creations unconditionally and equally. Unconditional love means "no conditions are set forth". God loves us no matter what. In God's eyes, everyone is special and no one is more special. God loves us all equally with a love we can only imagine.

It is time to trust ourselves to do our own thinking about what we read and what we experience in our lives. The process starts by questioning all of our beliefs...why we have come to believe them and do they reflect a God of love and joy, or one of fear and looking an awful lot like our earthly parents. Yes, doubt is the beginning of faith or finding a God we can rejoice in who does not terrorize us.

The Good News is a message that guilt and sinfulness have no place in our lives having understood that God loves us "no matter what." That will never change; so let us trade in the old god for a refreshing vision of God that we can truly take to our hearts. Then answer the question of who we think we are. We then understand that we are creations of that loving Father and like our Creator.

What does that mean for us? Remember to think for yourself on this. If what you come up with is joyful and makes you want to dance and rejoice, then you have discovered a God you can be close friends with; one who will welcome you with open arms.

Terry Lindsley,
Council Bluffs, Iowa; June 2017

Author's Note:
As you navigate through these pages, you may notice that the word, "God," is capitalized sometimes but not always. When capitalized, I am referring to the One Who Is, Always Was, and Always will be – in other words, the God who loves all of us unconditionally.

Where god is not capitalized, I am referring to the god of conditional love – an understanding that has served mankind throughout the centuries, but is now inadequate for these times. I believe the god who punishes, judges and lays out all kinds of conditions for us is not real and never was, only in the minds of church leaders and followers.

This rule of capitalization will make it easier to understand which concept of God I am talking about and no disrespect intended. The only exception is when the word God begins a sentence.

The Problem of Beliefs!

*You cannot discover new lands unless
you are willing to lose sight of the shore*
-Andre Gide

Nothing separates us as human beings as much as what our beliefs do. Beliefs can divide families, get us in trouble and cause a lot of tension in life. I am reminded that Jesus was crucified because he challenged the established and an entrenched belief system of the religious hierarchy. He died over a difference of opinion, so to speak. So differences in beliefs can be no small matter.

Belief systems are a collection of several beliefs that go together and paint a picture of how we see the world, others and ourselves. Examples of belief systems are prejudice, politics and religion. We join groups of like-minded people who hold the same or similar beliefs. Our beliefs are reinforced through what the group holds to be true. As a result our beliefs, being good or not so good, are confirmed by the group-think of that organization. It gives us security in adhering to the beliefs of the group. We become comfortable with our beliefs and as a result we don't think critically about them or, worse yet, never question them. So we take comfort in a group setting with others who give us the security of "being right," or may I say, "righteous," or being of a common mind. But happy is the person who is able to examine the underlying assumptions of his or her beliefs and discover a higher truth as they change.

Life experiences trump beliefs. An example is a racially prejudiced view is changed when a life experience clearly presents an opposing view, realizing that others we thought were inferior, lazy or freeloaders prove otherwise. We cannot paint all others of a certain group with the same brush and so our beliefs are often challenged by life's experience. A person who learns from life will question a prejudicial belief and see beyond a long held belief. Beliefs can and should evolve.

Many have questions about religious beliefs and the spiritual life. Religious beliefs especially are difficult to challenge. Being willing to look at what you believe and to have the courage to lay aside those beliefs that do not serve you anymore can be scary, but I can tell you that it is worth it. What awaits you on the other end of replacing some current beliefs with new ones is a joy and freedom you will not trade for anything. The God I hope you discover and come to know is the God who wants only our happiness and joy, freeing us from being a sinner, and of a life filled with fear. The alternative to a fear filled existence is a life filled with meaning and purpose. This is a personal journey to find your truth – what holds meaning for you. But it takes some courage. I am reminded of a quote: *"You cannot discover new lands unless you are willing to lose sight of the shore," – Andre Gide.* Again, this is the willingness to let go of some old beliefs and journey on to find new meaning.

Deciding to start: Trust yourself to navigate the world of beliefs and values to find the new meaning that starts to make sense of why you are here and what the world you live in is about. Help is available to anyone looking for answers. The key is that "you have to ask for it." Each of us has spiritual guides we can call on, the Holy Spirit, books and people all of whom will assist us in our search. Relax and put yourself in the hands of an all-loving God and don't be afraid. I would recommend that one of your daily prayers should include a prayer for "wisdom" on your journey. Then be aware of people, books and events that come into your life. They will have part of the answer you seek.

If you have questions about religious beliefs or are just trying to figure out what this life means, consider yourself blessed. That is the Holy Spirit working within you. Yes, you are being prodded to greater understanding and happiness. Two statements about faith apply here.

The first one states that the opposite of faith is "certainty." Those who feel they have all the answers have stopped asking questions and are no longer searching for "meaning." Certainty is their security. The answers they think they have may not reflect the God of unconditional love and following the rules will be their lot.

The second states that the beginning of faith is "doubt" or questioning. I would rather live on the side of uncertainty and have fun with the questions. I am confident that if I am questioning beliefs, then I am "alive spiritually." My wife, Barbara, and I both attest that we are more spiritually alive (I do not mean more "religious") than at any other time in our lives. I believe that it was the result of the Holy Spirit nudging us along with good questions and finding some answers along the way. Give your life and search to the Holy Spirit to guide you in this. You can trust none better and have confidence that you will find what is your truth and the beliefs you can live by.

How to start: Try to establish a morning routine that involves time spent in reading, prayer and reflection. It is a way of centering yourself as you begin your day. Perhaps open with a short prayer from the heart asking the Holy Spirit and your guides to direct you in your reading and reflection. Yes, you have to ask because God will never interfere with your free will. Select a book that provides thoughts for reflection. It doesn't have to be anything from any of the "sacred texts." Keep daily reading brief (1-3 pages maximum). Select something that poses one thought to think about. Then quiet your mind and ask the Holy Spirit to direct your "reflective time," that whatever communication takes place be only for your highest good. Take 10 minutes or so to reflect. End with a prayer of gratitude for this day, life and any other things to be grateful for. Remember to pray for wisdom on your journey.

Most of the time, this takes 15-30 minutes in the morning. If your morning routine is crowded with getting others and yourself ready for the day, perhaps rise a little earlier or figure a way to work it in. If you can share this time with a partner, what a blessing that is, but you can also do this on your own. You will find that starting your day this way keeps your spiritual senses alive and open to insights and opportunities.

What I described above is a starting point. What you discover through reflection will lead you to your truth. Each of us has lifetime guides, call them guardian angels if you like. The Holy Spirit and your guides will lead you to people, books and events that are relevant to your search and questioning. Trust them to be there for you. Listen to your thoughts during meditation or quiet time. I have had many books come my way at the right time more often than I can count that address my questions. People have come and gone from my life that provided insights, guidance and book recommendations. Live life with eyes and ears open and you will find the insights you are seeking. In our shared journey, Barbara and I have found the guidance to be right in line with the questions we had. We marvel at being the happiest and most peaceful in our golden years. We can look back and see that we were provided with what we needed when we were ready for it. The books listed under the appendix are good sources to start with. These have helped me clarify my beliefs and opened doors to living out of love instead of fear.

My Path: My path to spirituality is not your path. Each of us has a unique path from which we have learned and grown. I hope in this chapter to show how my beliefs were challenged and how they changed over the years to where I am less secure but much happier evaluating religious beliefs.

Before 1957 – Growing up: I attended a catholic grade school. During this time, I served as an altar boy for Masses and Novenas at my local parish. I felt that experience was otherworldly because many of the prayers were said in Latin with incense and bell ringing. I had admired my pastor and other priests I met in the process; I looked up to them.

I also attended a catholic high school where priests taught. During these years, I pondered what I wanted to do after high school and the priesthood was at the top of the list. My intentions were made known to the diocese and in my senior year. I knew I would be heading to a seminary. I was accepted to the seminary after graduation from high school in 1961. There I would get my degree in Philosophy, not one that screamed out "employment opportunities," but it certainly qualified as a college education and that was something. This is the kind of degree that teaches one how to think.

My time in college/seminary was a positive one. Benedictine monks taught and ran the school. During the summer months, I worked framing houses to save some spending money for the coming school year. If I ever had any notions of being special because of being a seminarian or studying for the priesthood, that job brought me back to the real world, but I enjoyed it. At the end of four years, I graduated with a B.A. in Philosophy; I now had my college degree.

Theological training: Upon graduating with my B.A. in Philosophy, I was headed to another seminary for my theological training. This seminary was quite different and much more regimented than the college seminary I attended. Daily newspapers were posted and certain articles were clipped out of them (which only heightened our curiosity). There was a very strict dress code. We were beginning the last phase of training for the active ministry. So I think the idea was that if we could get through the strict regimen of rules and restrictions, we'd be trained their way, would get used to following orders and regulations, and thus prepared for the active ministry.

It was also during my time here that I had a personal belief crisis. We were being schooled specifically in theology. In studying one of the earlier theologians, perhaps St. Augustine, God was defined by a series of numbers based on the doctrine of the Trinity. So the thinking was that there was 1-God, 2-natures, 3-persons, and 4 of something else I can't recall right now. This was not a god I could relate to. This concept was meaningless to me. It was empty of content, but it apparently meant something to someone centuries ago. I was beginning to question other things as well and wondering if this was what I really wanted to do.

At the time, I was trying to sprout a philodendron in my room. It didn't seem to be doing anything, but it wasn't dying either. I returned from a home visit and all kinds of roots had sprouted. Call me crazy, but I took that as a sign to hang in there. I got past that crisis and my studies and life became more meaningful.

Steps to the priesthood were ordination to the Sub-Diaconate, and the Diaconate. These occurred in the last two years of training. By the time of graduation, we had all learned to say Mass in both English and Latin -

(This was just after the Second Vatican Council which authorized Mass to be said in the native language). We practiced with our backs to the congregation. Yes, it was a miracle that I made it through. I was one of the rebels of the group. It was in 1969 that this seminary closed its doors. We were the last class to graduate from there.

Active Ministry: Ordination ceremony was held on May 25th, 1969. My first Mass was held at my home parish with the pastor and other co-celebrants participating. I think my parents breathed a sigh of relief that with all the ups and downs, they now had a priest in the family.

Upon ordination, we were ready for our first assignment; mine was to a small rural parish, where an aging pastor needed some assistance over the summer months. The pastor had been at that parish for 42 years.

My next assignment was a large city parish - (Fall of 1969). It was an adjustment from the small parish with much larger attendance at Masses, etc. Being a young priest, I had a lot to learn but I always welcomed a learning opportunity.

It was during my sixth year in the active ministry that I seriously contemplated leaving. I was becoming more and more dissatisfied with the party line or the politics of the Church and seriously questioned if I would be happy continuing on this path. I looked around at the priests who were older and out in small parishes. Some had alcohol problems and, I felt they were basically lonely. I wondered what my later years as a priest might be like. This proved to be one of the big decisions of my life. In hindsight, it was the right one.

During this time, I turned to journaling – putting my feelings and thoughts on paper. It proved to be a useful tool. I do not underestimate journaling. It is therapeutic. I worked through resentments and other baggage around that decision and left with little anger and no long-term resentments. Looking back on my journaling during that year, I saw a lot of anger surfacing and by the end of the year I had pretty much reached a decision.

The first task was to tell my parents. They were so proud to have a priest in the family. I knew that it would hit them hard. They listened to me and heard me out. I remember one of Dad's comments that I had a job with security; why would I want to leave that? True as that might be, I would have been miserable in the long run. Part of my decision was that I wanted to keep marriage as an option in the future. This came at a time when many priests were leaving the active ministry in the early 70's.

In 1975, I approached my Bishop and shared my decision. Being the caring man that he was, he wanted me to be sure and recommended I make a several day retreat before coming to a final decision. I honored his request. It didn't change my decision. So in the summer of 1975 I packed my bags and left the active ministry. By this time, my parents had already relocated in a nearby state. They had room for me to live there. That was a godsend as I began looking for work. All I knew was that my skill set was in working with people.

After priesthood: At 33 years old, most of my peers were well launched in their careers, and I had to find a new one. I worked at a series of jobs, a short stint at a dry cleaner's, and a year at a residential children's home as a house parent.

It was during this time that I met my future life partner, Barbara. She was active in the church and we met at a meeting. She was in the process of a divorce and I was getting my feet on the ground as a civilian. We both had some things we needed to work through before getting into a serious relationship.

In 1977 we were both in a good position and our relationship had grown. We started looking at property to buy and found a six-acre plot of land in the city that had a house and some out buildings. Barbara and I and three of her children moved onto the property in August of 1977. This turned out to be a great nurturing environment to raise a family. However, I needed to know if the children would be accepting of that arrangement, so we lived together. By Christmas of that year, the children presented me with a very welcomed gift of "adoption papers" – yes, they were adopting me into the family. With that question resolved, Barbara and I were married on Oct. 7th, 1978. An ex-priest performed the ceremony on our home property. Do we do anything traditionally?

There was a lot of pain for my parents during the first year after the wedding. They did not attend the wedding ceremony. It was in November of 1979 that Barbara called my mom and invited them over for Thanksgiving dinner; they accepted. That was the beginning of a healing that needed to happen. When dad passed away in 1985, healing had taken place and we had reconciled any hurts of the past.

As well as raising a family, Barb and I found time to get involved with other things. It was during this time that Barbara and I were both National Red Cross instructors in disaster classes. Her specialty was teaching others to be trainers and I taught a class that prepared workers going out into the field on how to relate to people of differing backgrounds, language, cultures, values, etc., called, "Serving the Diverse Community." In 1983, I took a job with Job Training Partnership Act (JTPA), a federal job-training program as a caseworker. Barbara got a job at the School for the Deaf. We were also active severe weather spotters for the National Weather Service and both had our ham radio licenses.

The JTPA program came to an end in 2000 and a new job-training program was being introduced that year. I decided to retire at the end of the old program. This was my first retirement and it lasted about a year. I was not looking for full-time employment but a part-time opening with the local County Emergency Management Agency was available. With my Red Cross disaster background, I got the job.

Mom passed away in 2010 at the age of 93, twenty-five years after Dad. Now it was my brother, sister and I who were to carry on with the family. None of us had any children of our own, but Barbara with her three of the eight children filled a void for Mom during those years and ours were her adopted grandchildren. She remembered their birthdays and attended their parties, and was involved in their lives.

During this time, Barbara and I were volunteering at a local hospital. I was still with Emergency Management. In 2012, the agency decided to cut funding for my position so I decided to retire for a second time.

It was that same year that I spoke with the head chaplain at our hospital. She was looking for someone to help with the on-call chaplain program. I didn't have any Clinical Pastoral Education, which she preferred, but as a priest some 40+ years ago, I had training working with the sick and the dying. She decided to take a risk with me. And now six years later, I have learned a lot from that experience. The staff seems satisfied with my work at the hospital. I find the role of chaplain meaningful and it gives me a lot to think about.

In 2009, Barb and I and another hospital volunteer started the 'No One Dies Alone' program at the hospital with a team of nine. This team sits with patients who have no family or friends locally and who are in "end of life care." We also do a monthly used book sale in the hospital lobby and help out with fundraisers there. So through these activities, we established a spiritual connection with the hospital community.

In September of 2016, I had a kidney stone attack. The CT scan at the hospital revealed a couple enlarged lymph nodes. The kidney stone issue was resolved, but the lymph nodes needed to be investigated. So in January of 2017 at age 74, I had to take a medical leave for chemotherapy cancer treatments for non-Hodgkins lymphoma. A PT scan on June 6th, 2017 showed the cancer was in remission and I returned to the hospital work in July.

The bottom line in all this is that I have been guided to be able to do the work I am doing. The path I have traveled is unique to me. Life events have helped to define my life today; but I believe that things happen for a reason. Look back and trust your path in life and see where things could have gone all wrong, but didn't. Or perhaps things did all go terribly wrong and that proved to be a wake-up call you needed. I've had both of those. Life's experiences shape us all. My beliefs have changed over time thanks to my ability to question everything. As Marianne Williamson would coach us to lift our hearts to heaven in gratitude and say, *"I honor my past. It is what got me here."*[1]

The theme of not judging what others are doing also applies on a broad scale to the many other world religions and faith traditions. It is easy to play the game of spiritual "specialness" saying ours is a better way. *A Course in Miracles* cautions us not to take another's path as our own, but neither should we judge it. We should just keep in mind that the Holy Spirit is working with all God's children in all religious traditions. If God is Love, then we need to recognize love in all its human costumes and rejoice that it is so.

The next chapter examines various beliefs about God. Having a good foundational belief about God is the basis of everything that we believe.

---

[1] A Return to Love by Marianne Williamson (c. 1962) p. 71

About God

*Once we get this right,
the rest falls into place.*

This chapter is crucial to understanding and analyzing our concept of God. It really comes down to two choices and we have been exposed to both. But which one is at the core of our belief system? The issue is this: God is love, but which kind of love? God is perceived as one of "conditional love" or "unconditional" love. That is the choice. What does all that mean, and why is it so important?

It is important because it is a starting point for all that comes later. In all theologies, this is the starting point. If the assumptions at the starting point are erroneous, then the error in thinking becomes huge as time goes on and more baggage is added onto it. Almost all religious texts contain passages of the conditional god of love. And with time whole belief systems and worship are built to support this concept.

But a good starting point can expand and excite anyone's spirituality by opening up a whole new world of God's love as unconditional. This can work for Hindu, Muslim, Seventh-Day Adventists, and any other religious belief system. It is that basic. I am proposing the proper underpinnings or assumptions of any theology for today and future spirituality's. This will be the first "belief" challenge for those who question what they believe. This is key and basic to the new spirituality. Get this right and the rest is easy. Now for some background information:

For centuries, the concept of this world was very narrow. I call it the "flat-earth" world-view. Yes, the people of the world and the Catholic Church all believed at one time that the earth was flat and that the sun revolved around the earth. The sun was in a layer above the earth along with the stars that rotated around this flat earth. There was a third layer above that where God lived and where Heaven existed. So theoretically, the earth would have had corners and edges somewhere. This explanation seemed to satisfy the masses and that was how they conceived their world and the universe. It was a very limited view and they were the center of it all. God created this all for us!

However, Galileo and some others (@1500 CE) challenged this limiting world-view by changing where we were in all this. We were no longer at the center of it all. We now revolved around the sun and there were other planets that did the same. As we now know, our view of the universe is unlimited and we are but a speck of sand on the beach of the universe, so to speak. How much more expansive is this, more amazing than the flat-Earth view could have ever given us. Yes, the earth-people today share a wonderful, very large system of creation likely with other intelligent beings.

I use these examples to begin a discussion of the two ways we conceptualize God. One is a limiting view and the other an expansive, inclusive and accepting view. Now for a deeper look into these two views.

The god of Conditional Love: The god of "conditional love" is still taught in Sunday schools, pulpits and on the airwaves. This god is called the "theistic" view of our creator and it was an effective tool for keeping everyone in line and in the church. Growing up in a Catholic school I can tell you that the "god of conditional love," the one that I was exposed to was drilled into my religious education. In short, it was always "god will love you if...." we had to earn divine love! Something like Santa Claus, god knew all and all that we had done in our lifetime. This would be brought to light after we breathed our last breath and stood before the judgment seat of our creator to account for what we did or didn't do. A judgment made at that time would determine for "eternity" our fate of either heaven or hell. There were many rules and guidelines interpreted by men over the history of the Catholic Church that reflected this concept. God was to be feared – period. This fear of god was reflected in rules that stated a Catholic could not receive communion at Mass if a serious sin was committed. A person had to go to Confession or receive the Sacrament of Penance to be forgiven and reinstated in a "graceful' state. Eating meat on Fridays was something that could condemn a person to hell for all eternity and you only had to do it once. It was a serious sin to miss Mass on Sundays and holydays of obligation if you were healthy and able to attend. If you left the fold, salvation would not be found outside of the Catholic Church. The classic one for me was the one that stated a kiss over 60 seconds was a serious sin, but one hundred 59 second kisses were not. It reminded me of counting calories when being on a diet. We were always in a battle with the devil in this life.

Confirmation was a sacrament whereby we were made soldiers for Christ to fight for the good and against evil. Life was not too complicated but a lot of our decisions were based on fear. You just had to know the rules, e.g.: the Ten Commandments. Motivation for being good and loving came from outside – are we following the Ten Commandments or not? There are many more examples of this, but these illustrate that earning god's love always had "conditions." The Bible is full of this kind of portrayal of god, especially the Old Testament. There was plenty of material for any Sunday school lesson, sermon or radio/TV show from which to draw. There was the implication that god could be disappointed in us and saddened by our decisions and behaviors. This god had emotions much like our earthly parents and rendered punishments, etc. Of course, one did not want to disappoint the creator. It is no wonder that people on their deathbed were afraid to die fearing eternal punishments and recalling regrets in life. In fairness, many of the negative laws based on the theistic concept of god that were in force when I was growing up, are not emphasized as much in the Catholic church today, but neither is the God of unconditional love the core of the faith.

Traditional Worship: Nowhere is this concept of "conditional love" more evident than in the Church's ritual liturgies or religious services. One of the first things we do at Mass is to recognize our sinfulness and failures and ask god to "have mercy on us," not once but many times throughout the ceremony. We come kneeling and groveling at the feet of our savior asking him to look favorably on us. Many congregations now have "Praise Teams" whereby we praise god for being all-powerful and appeasing our deity with prayers and songs of praise. God does not need to be told how great "thou art." He knows him/herself. With this view, we believe that ours is a fallen nature and in need of redemption. As the account relates, it took Jesus, god's only begotten son to incarnate 2000 years ago. Through his death, mankind was redeemed from an impossible situation. Man could not accomplish this. It required divine intervention. This is just one area that the theistic concept seems to need rethinking. It doesn't seem to relate to us today.

Atheism, a clarification: Atheism is often taken to mean that a person does not believe in God or a god. Really the term can be taken to mean that a person does not believe in a "theistic" god. They may believe in God other than the theistic idea of god. I am an atheist then. I don't accept the theistic definition or description of god, but I am definitely a firm believer in the God of unconditional love. So what's that about?

The God of Unconditional Love: This theistic god just described above, died for me some time ago and I question if a god like that ever existed. It was just our belief in that god that persisted. If a person rejects this notion of god, creator, supreme being and judge, then what other concepts of God are out there? How else could we think about God?

One of the jewels of the New Testament that illustrates this perfectly is the parable of the Prodigal Son in Luke 15:11. This comes directly from Jesus as the source. It paints perfectly a different picture of a God of Love. To summarize, one of a man's two sons asks for his portion of his inheritance, leaves home and separates himself from his family, takes the money and runs. He soon goes through the money and finds himself feeding a farmer's pigs for a job. He comes to his senses and decides that he will return and make amends with his family and take whatever job his father has for him. He will bite the bullet and return home and take his licks. He has his apology all thought out and as he approaches his family home, the father sees him coming while still far out. He orders a celebration in his returning son's honor. He doesn't wait for reconciliation to take place. The son is welcomed back without any conditions. The son was the treasure. I believe this is a more accurate description of the God who IS. Punishment, vengeance, retribution and judgment are NOT attributes of God. God is pure, unconditional love. God loves us no matter what we do, say or believe.

Now this is a quantum leap of faith. Having been schooled and trained in the theistic concept, there were a lot of questions that I had to wrestle with concerning this concept of an unconditional loving God. Does that mean that even the worst of humanity is loved regardless of what they do? Then if I am loved, why bother with rules? Go ahead and live it up! God won't care! It doesn't seem fair that I try to live a life of virtue while others don't when we are all loved anyway. What about hell? What is the book of Revelation all about then? That doesn't seem to jive with an all-loving God. Why would Jesus' second coming be so different from his first? In the theistic way of thinking, things could either be explained or were a "mystery."

These are just a few of many questions that I had to work through. But the good news is that in this concept, there is no "fear of God." Once that fear is gone, we experience the freedom to be truly sons and daughters of our Creator and letting the Creator's love shine through us. Our joy returns and a passion for making loving decisions is not based on fear.

If God is not judging us for what we have done, then who is held accountable: That would have to be "us." (This will be further explained in chapter six.) God gave us free will and a loving God will not interfere with our decisions. We can't blame anyone else. Does that mean that there is no place called hell? How do we hold ourselves accountable for our actions? There are other concepts that explain and answer the many questions people have when adopting this concept of God. These were never talked about in religious education or in church, yet they all make sense in becoming comfortable with believing in an all loving God, who created us in his image and likeness. It has to do with spiritual psychology or what we know now about the soul and its desire to evolve through the experiences of earthly lifetimes. This may seem hard to believe and another leap of faith, but stay with me. This will be explained in later chapters and in much more detail, but the bottom line is that we hold ourselves accountable and learn from each lifetime experience. It is not God who makes decisions about what was done. We do with the love and guidance on the other side of the veil after we die. It makes sense to me that a God of unconditional love would overlook our misdeeds and love the good things we did. Love does not interfere with free will. Our God is a patient and loving God, not a jealous god.

The insight that many Christians miss is that the New Law that Jesus revealed is distinctly different from the Ten Commandments. Instead of revealing ten more rules to follow, he shows us that WE need to determine what it means to love and grow in a world that is so often based on "unloving" decisions that are made all around us. That puts the responsibility squarely on our shoulders. No more outside rules to follow. No more excuses. All of a sudden, what being a Christian means is more challenging because we have to decide what "loving" means. Motivation is coming from within and not from a set of external rules.

Evolving Worship: This is an area that begs to be explored. A new concept of God means changes in the way we worship. Current rituals in churches do not reflect the love of an "unconditional God." There are some experimental models that eliminate any guilt and fear. In coming together in community to celebrate God's unconditional love for all, scripture readings, songs and sermons about guilt and fear would be eliminated. What's left when guilt, groveling and fear is eliminated? The new liturgies would be characterized by joy, celebrating God's undying love for us. There could be personal testimony from one of those assembled as to how they have experienced the hand of God in their life. You would never hear in this service that "Jesus died for my sins." Instead of "Praise Teams," a proper title would be "Awe Teams" with songs and readings reflecting our deep gratitude and awe for being in God's presence. People who have died and come back to tell about it (Near Death Experiences) remarkably relate that when meeting Jesus, there was no fear but a genuine sense of awe, admiration, peace and acceptance. All in the congregation should come together in gratitude and appreciation. Our response in the presence of God should be one of awe vs. praise, true humility and total acceptance instead of groveling and begging for divine mercy. Kneeling, a sign of submission would be eliminated. Only Bible readings that reflect the "Good News" would be selected for a service. Other passages that foster guilt and fear of God would not be read. Readings could include sources outside of the Bible that reflect God's revelation today and there are many that could be used. (Yes, God's revelation continues today as seen in later chapters). Along with helping a congregation understand the new, an ongoing class including the most recent Biblical scholarship should be an integral part of a congregation's mission. The liturgies of the future would also reflect our understanding of whom we are (discussed in the next chapter) and our relationship to an all-loving Father.

Recently, my wife, Barbara, had a discussion with a relative who related a "near-death-experience." He said he had died and before he was revived, he had the realization that he was totally engulfed in an intelligent all loving presence. He heard what he claimed was the voice of God say to him, *"Everything will be all right. I love you no matter what!"* There are no conditions for God's eternal love for us.

Bishop Desmond Tutu shared an insight:

There is nothing you can do to make God love you more, for God already loves you perfectly and totally. But more wonderfully, there is nothing you can do to make God love you less - absolutely nothing, for God already loves you and will love you forever.[1]

Unconditional love means love with no judgment. My wife and I and a team participate in a hospital program called 'No One Dies Alone'. We attend the dying that has no family or friends during their last 36-48 hours of life. The team's main message to the dying is one of hope, one of a God whose love for them is unconditional, love without judgment. Whatever regrets or failures of their lives will not matter when they meet their Creator. The message is positive and reassuring.

Is God changing or is our understanding of God changing: When I was in the active ministry, I remember to this day hearing a homily with the message, "God is always bigger than we think He is." To me, this simply means there is always more to know about the One whose image and likeness we reflect.

We as human beings always want to put a face on God – someone we can relate to – a person or personality. When he walked the earth, Jesus was the face of our Father. Today, new understandings of God are taking root that challenge our whole thinking about the God Who IS. God has not changed over the centuries, but man's understanding of God has. In the Old Testament god watched over His chosen people and would protect them in battle, etc. This was a tribal god. Then that understanding evolved to one that looked beyond the tribe to include other peoples and more of a god for all peoples. But this god still had a lot of conditions to be met before mankind could gain his favor. A later understanding called for us to love our "enemies." Still later understandings included a God who loves unconditionally – simply put – God is LOVE and no one can be "un-loved." But there may be even a much bigger understanding that is emerging that describes God not as a being, but as Being itself. There is the expression today that we can interact with the forces of the universe. The Law of Attraction methodology works with this concept. It might be that our new understanding of God is that His presence is everywhere – within others, the whole vast universe and us. This does away with a God who is a person or personality, but something that we are part of and connected to, an intelligent loving presence. This radically changes the way God is traditionally understood, but the Biblical idea that God is Love is still true. Anyway, can we pray to Being itself? God is always bigger than we think. People with all these different concepts of God will surely pray differently from each other. Where does your concept of God fit in all of this?

I do not attempt to define God or pretend to know how to characterize our Creator but only to say that God's love is clearly unconditional, whoever or whatever

God is. I think man is incapable of "defining God." But these are some thoughts I offer that are being talked about this day. The basic choice between seeing God's love as conditional or "with conditions" or unconditional is the key question for all of us. Which choice we make will determine the basis of our theology – how we talk and think about God. This is the first and fundamental choice for us all.

This is as far as I intend to go with this discussion because it is so basic to everything else that follows. If it resonates with you, then the Holy Spirit will work with you to further your understanding of unconditional love. Remember you have to ask for that help. He'll never fail you and the world you'll discover will amaze you. I can't emphasize enough to pray daily for wisdom and insight.

I opted to see God as unconditional love some 30 years ago. It answers so many questions that the theistic or the typical religious story didn't address. In subsequent chapters, I hope to show how when properly understood this concept of God gives each of us hope and eliminates the fear of death. It makes a much better fit for our understanding of our God, us and the world we live in. The theistic approach is dying a slow death and the new emerging story offers a wider vision of all of the above. I am so much at peace with an "unconditional loving God," the new understanding that is catching on in our time. We struggle to understand how much God loves us because there is no example in our experience that we can fully understand this.

If the goal of this lifetime for me was to come from the theistic approach to this new understanding, then I have had a productive life. Life is fun and joyful again free of fear and full of hope and possibilities.

If you have followed this text so far, then the next chapter tackles the question of who we are and how we relate to the real God of unconditional love.

---

[1] God Has A Dream by Bishop Desmond Tutu (c. 2005) p. 32

About Jesus and All of Us

*You are not what you have been told
and you are more than you ever imagined.*
- Gregg Braden

Now that an appreciation of a God of unconditional love is in place, the next big question is "Who are we?" This is not a trivial question and the way it has been addressed throughout the ages has not helped to answer that question. How we answer this one question will affect everything we do in life. There is no more important question than this one. How we answer relates directly to our concept of God.

The God of conditional love and us: If we use the conditional love version of god, then we define and describe ourselves as follows:
- We are sinners and in need of redemption.
- We are here on earth to prove ourselves worthy of a heavenly reward.
- We are a fallen nature.
- If we incur god's disfavor, this can be serious and have implications for all eternity.
- The god of conditional love can be offended and angered.
- Thinking that we were anything more than miserable sinners was heresy.

- This god was exclusive; you could either be on the inside and be "saved" or on the outside of that special group or worse excommunicated from the church.
- We are here to please god.
- Punishment and guilt for transgressions was always hanging over our heads.

This is a centuries old understanding that we grew up believing. It carried with it tons of guilt.

The God of unconditional love and us: If we use the concept of a God of unconditional love, then we define ourselves differently:

- We are created in God's image and likeness. We have God-like qualities.
- We are all precious children of our Father and loved unconditionally.

We are here on earth so that our soul (who we are) can evolve and learn life lessons. These life lessons have to do with ourselves and other souls we interact with. We are all here for this purpose.

As mentioned before, one of the pearls of wisdom found in the New Testament is the parable of the Prodigal Son. What he had done didn't matter. The son was the

> *The reason why God does not interfere with man's free will is that that is the ultimate in respect, and God does respect His creations even though His creations don't. If He interfered with their will, He would be enslaving them and God does not enslave.*
> *- Ken Wapnick*

treasure and his return was reason for rejoicing. Admittedly, I had a hard time getting my arms around this concept after living with a god of conditional love for much of my younger years. But in the end, it makes so much sense that an all-accepting God comes closest to a healthy understanding of our Creator, Father. This God cannot be angered and loves us no matter what – no matter what. We are all His precious children. It does not seem fair somehow. What about those who are out there screwing up big time with their lives being a mess and not reflecting the presence of the love of God?

Well, our Creator gave us the gift of free will, the ability to make choices. Some of us will make good ones and others won't. Those that make harmful decisions are not "bad" souls; they are good souls who have lost their way in this lifetime. Mistakes can be corrected. It may take another lifetime or more to get it right. There is nothing that we can say, think or do that will diminish in any way, the Father's incredible love for us. Again, God is Love and we should have no fear or guilt in our minds about God. Jesus showed us the Father when he was here on earth. He befriended the most notorious sinners of his time. He accepted them much to the chagrin of the religious officials of his time.

So who or what are we?
- Some say we are created in the image and likeness of God. That must mean that we have God-like qualities.
- Some maintain that we are spirits having a human experience. This earth is not our

permanent home. We are temporary residents here.
- Others say that we are all part of a collective of all God's created souls that together is called the "Sonship." We are all children of the Father.

All three reveal clues about who we are. Those who have had near-death-experiences, or died and have been revived tell us what they experienced. We learn that they experienced being engulfed in unconditional love. They also conveyed that we are much more than we realize. We are all "magnificent beings." We are as God created us, and precious in His sight. We are all His cherished children. This realization was validated when people shared their near-death experiences. Yes, we even have God-like attributes. We have the potential to do even greater things than Jesus is recorded to have done. But our memories of our potential have been dulled and we have a hard time realizing this. We are conscious spiritual beings at our cores. We have incarnated to have a human experience so we can learn life lessons and evolve or become more loving reflecting our Father's love to others. That is what the human

> *In God's family, there are no outsiders. All are insiders. Black and white, rich and poor, gay and straight, Jew and Arab, Palestinian and Israeli, Serb and Albanian, Hutu and Tutsi, Muslim and Christian, Buddhist and Hindu, Pakistani and Indian -all belong.*
>
> **Bishop Desmond Tutu**

experience is for. We are all here to learn something that we decided on before we were born.

The Sonship and Jesus: This concept of the Sonship needs some explanation. In 325 CE, the Council of Nicea was convened. A burning issue at that time questioned who Jesus was. Jesus was either the only begotten Son of the Father, or was he a very enlightened soul that incarnated to bring an important message to mankind. There was much bitter debate over this issue. The final decision was that Jesus was the "only-begotten Son of God the Father." Unfortunately, this mistaken notion has persisted for 1700 years. We still recite the Nicene Creed in our worship services to this day. But Jesus seems to tell us a different story. He tells us that he was one of us, our brother, and no more God-like than we are. In John 14:12 Jesus is quoted as saying:

> *Truly, truly I say to you, he who believes in me will do the works that I do; and greater works than these he will do, because I go to the Father.*

In A Course of Love, Jesus, speaking in the first person says:

> *I did not proclaim myself to be above or different from the rest, but called each of you brother and sister and reminded you of our Father's love and our union with Him.*[1]

Now if we want to use the analogy of the Trinity (Father, Son & Holy Spirit), then we, and Jesus as the collective of the Father's children are the Sonship. This could be properly understood as we all comprise the second person of the Blessed Trinity with God-like qualities. This is a new understanding of our relationship with God, but one that resonates with me. I now try to see myself and every other person as a precious child of our Father. This is what we have in common. Each of us is here to learn our life lessons and to help each other. We cannot attempt to judge another's life or behavior because we don't begin to understand what their life is about. What a relief to know that the burden of judging has been lifted from our shoulders! With this new understanding, it might well be heresy to think of ourselves as miserable sinners and not worthy of God's love.

The Sonship Expanded: So far, I've described the Sonship in terms of this planet and its history. It seems that the universe is teaming with life. It would be reasonable to assume so and for the sake of asking the next question, let's assume so. If there are other civilizations and sentient beings on other planets throughout the universe, and there is but one God of the universe, what of them? Surely they are also children of our Creator as well and part of the grand Sonship as are we. They likely were visited by an advanced soul like Jesus was for us. Are they also our brothers and sisters? It is fascinating to take theological assumptions and apply them to the universe. Here again, God is always bigger than we think.

The answer to our true identity has changed through history. Early man without a sacred text to provide any clues had to observe their existence and put together a cultural story that made sense to them and their tribe. Many early religions have their own story of origin as the Bible does - the story of the Garden of Eden. Just as man's view of the universe progressed from the flat earth theory to the expansive universe of today, so has the answer to the question of "who are we?" Now more than ever, mankind needs to be open to new explanations of our relationship with God. Not to examine this basic belief is to remain stuck with an outdated and inaccurate belief that doesn't serve mankind well today.

We are an integral part of God and God of us. This is the new understanding and is quite a break from the understanding of the past. That story told us that we are separate from God; that God lived outside of us and that one day we could be united again in heaven.

Separation from God: *A Course in Miracles* states that we really have only one problem and that is we believe we are separated from God. Indeed, it goes even further that we believe that we are separate from each other. We all have bodies that are distinctly separate. We see each other as individuals. But there is a reality that says that we are not separate from God or each other.

This took some time for me to understand, but I share my current limited understanding here. This concept is a work in progress. It has a lot to say about who we are! We are a part of the magnificent Sonship of the Father. That is one thing we have in common, but there is more. The very life that animates our bodies, our souls, is God-like, the God force. We all have that in common no matter how bad we think we are. We owe our existence to the divine life force that is part of us. Each of us is an individuation of this divine presence. Although we appear to be separate from each other, we are all connected in another sense.

Marianne Williamson provides an analogy to illustrate this in her book, A Return To Love using the analogies of the ocean:

> *Waves are not separate from the ocean but are part of the ocean. Waves could be perceived separately but in reality all waves are part of the larger reality, the ocean. To continue the analogy, each of us are a wave on the larger ocean of God's creation.* [2]

This is our reality and has been all along. It suggests a whole new way of how we see each other and how we treat each other. As we see ourselves is how we see others and the world we live in. So it makes a difference in what we call each other. Are we all brothers and sisters and are we not of the same family? We have to be careful not to demonize others and see them as enemies. It is hard to see fellow family members as an "enemy." We are all good souls, but some have lost their way and don't see things this way. That is one way of explaining evil in the world.

Another illustration of this concept involves something anyone can do. First with your right hand, cover the left hand so that only the fingers show. Each moves independently of the others and seem to be separate until you remove your right hand to reveal that all the fingers are indeed part of that hand. They share a common identity and without the hand, they are nothing and have no life of their own.

Anita Moorjani also had insight with her Near-Death Experience (NDE):

> *Out of the many messages I brought back from my NDE – we are all one, we are love at our core, we are magnificent – this was the strongest one and kept reverberating with me.*[3]

This concept alone can be the subject of many a morning meditation to arrive at a more accurate idea of who we are and who we are in relationship to our Creator. So how we talk about this relationship to our fellow sons and daughters in the Sonship is important.

To recap the quote that begins this chapter, *"You are not what you have been told, and you are more than you ever imagined,"* was not a concept I grew up with but one that is growing in me. It is a much more expansive concept of self than I had before.

We need each other to attain salvation or to advance in our soul's evolution.

A Course in Miracles addresses this matter:

> *You forsake yourself and God if you forsake any of your brothers. You must learn to see them as they are, and understand they belong to God as you do. How could you treat your brother better than by rendering unto God the things that are God's?*[4]

As our understanding of who God is has expanded throughout history, so our self-concept also had to change over time. If we can grasp this concept, this lifetime will have been a great leap forward in our soul's evolution.

What complicates our understanding or our relationship with God is the problem of the Sacred Text we use. That "book" often confuses the "people of the book".

---

[1] A Course of Love, (c. 2014) p. 132
[2] A Return To Love, by Marianne Williamson, (c. 1992), p. 29
[3] Dying to be Me, by Anita Moorjani, (c. 2012), p. 113
[4] A Course in Miracles, Foundation for Inner Peace, (c. 1977), T-5 IV:6, Text p. 82

4

People of the Book

*Being tied to one "Sacred Text"
excludes seeing Divine revelation today.*

Throughout history, there have been many "sacred texts" or documents that were used by groups or organized religions as a guide in their spiritual journey. As I found out in examining many of these, they come with truth and inspiration along with other passages that are contradictory and counter-productive. I will keep this simple! As you read the Bible, the Book of Mormon, the Koran, to name just a few, you find passages that clearly depict God as a god of "conditional" love. You will also find a few that show God's love to be "unconditional." That is how I look at any sacred text and see what it has to offer me in my path. What if churches just took passages that reflected our Creator's true nature of unconditional love and occasionally shared a reading from a different source other than the one they swear by? When we attend church services, we expect to hear readings from the one time proven guiding text that has directed that faith tradition and not from any other source.

All religions suffer from this malady. They insist on being tied to one source as their exclusive guide. Some condemn other faith traditions and the books they follow. To say that every word in the Bible and many other sacred texts is the Word of God is almost impossible to defend. People would like to have that false security, but the books don't support it. Not every word and text in the Book qualifies as God's Word. At a minimum, maybe we should just take the texts of wisdom and read those and dismiss the texts of guilt and sin.

Every religion has struggled to understand a God who loves without conditions. Most sacred texts feel they have to interpret what God wants from us. This reflected in the prescribed norms for worship, rules of conduct and religious laws and customs.

Just for a moment, imagine yourself sitting in your usual Sunday church service and hearing the reader announce the reading, "Today's first reading is taken from *A Course in Miracles*." You think to yourself, "Am I in the right church? Did I take a wrong turn somewhere? What's going on here?" And so the reader gives the reading and at the end the congregation is supposed to say, "This is the Word of the Lord." Would you be able to respond, "Thanks be to God?"

Your first questions might likely be "Why? This isn't right. Who planned this liturgy anyway?" Your next question could be, "Why not?" Why not hear the wisdom of some of the other "sacred texts" used by other faiths? After all, wisdom is wisdom just as love is love wherever we find it.

Bishop Desmond Tutu has noted, "Not everything in the Bible has lasting value."[1] The same can be said for other sacred texts. The Bible is a very misunderstood work and deserves a closer look.

The Holy Bible: In 325 CE, the formal canon of the Bible was determined. At that time, there were many spiritual texts that existed some of which we now have through the discovery of the Dead Sea scrolls. The books of the Bible that we have today were written between 1000 BCE and 130 CE.

The New Testament is a reflective experience of first century Christians. St. Paul writes from 51 to 64 CE when he died, "Not all of the epistles attributed to him were authored by him." The latest "Pauline" work is dated @ 130 CE or 100 years after the death of Jesus. So obviously, some were not written by Paul but perhaps by his followers. Many believe that the Gospels were eyewitness accounts of the life of Jesus. The Gospels were written from @70 to 100 CE. The authors of the Gospels were not contemporaries of Jesus, but wrote 40 to 60 years after his death. So believing that the Gospels are personal witness to the events in the life of Jesus might be misleading. Paul never mentions the virgin birth, the miracles Jesus worked or his ascension. These first appear in the Gospels and were added by the authors. When listing the names of the twelve apostles, the lists are not consistent; they differ in their account of who the twelve were. Besides some inconsistencies like these, there are three big problems that the Bible has:

First, to believe that every word in the Bible is the inspired Word of God can hardly be supported because there are contradictions. God's Word is consistent and free of contradictions.

Second, the Bible is ambiguous about who God is. God is often portrayed as a God of conditional love – *I will love you if you keep my commandments and there will be consequences if you don't*. But there are also passages that describe very eloquently a God of unconditional love – the Prodigal Son for example. The Bible does contain the Word of God, but a lot of it is also not. Because the Bible often shows God coming in and punishing the wicked or that the wicked get their due, we figure that by imitating God, we can do that also. So the Bible has been used to justify slavery, wars and discrimination just to name a few. When I read the Bible, my impression is mostly that our god is one of "conditional" love. A God of unconditional love is not vindictive, judgmental or punishing. My personal belief is that God's love is unconditional therefore many of the Bible readings do not resonate with me, but in fairness, there are many that do.

Third, a major problem in understanding the message of the Bible is that we take it literally, like all the events described actually happened. The Jewish people saw more the moral of the story rather than actual details around what happened. Some have suggested that the miracles that Jesus performed may not have actually happened; it was the point of the story that mattered. When the Bible texts were taken to the gentiles, or non-

Jewish people, they assumed the accounts were historical. For some believing Christians, who take the Bible literally today, if Jesus worked no miracles, their faith would be shaken. It is not a deal breaker for me either way. The message and teachings of Jesus are what he was about.

Some fundamentalist Bible scholars have even gone to great lengths to make predictions because they were so sure they found evidence in the Bible only to be embarrassed when the time came and went with nothing happening as predicted. I saw that clearly stated on a billboard in 2011: "Have you heard the Awesome news? The End of the World begins on May 21, 2011. The Bible guarantees it!" These were seen in several major U.S. cities. Every religion has a group that insists on interpreting their book and sticking with the fundamentals. These basic tenets are often rigid and tend to be put forth as sticking with a 2000-year-old message regardless of how the times change. Out of this fundamentalism are extremists born when the rest of the world seems to be leaving them behind.

Bible Study groups: I shudder inside when someone tells me that they are part of a Bible study group. I wonder if the guide they are using includes the latest Biblical scholarship and what we know about the Bible today. I suspect that a lot of these texts still present Jesus as the only begotten Son of God and that He died for our sins. This is accompanied by a boatload of guilt, especially when studying the Book of Revelation, which is a popular topic in view of the times we live in. Are instructors extrapolating interpretations for today from that book? It was a controversial book to begin with and there was a lot of debate over whether or not to even include it in the final Canon of the Bible. It is really a book set in a time when there was imminent threat from the Roman Empire and it was written from the viewpoint of the Christian community at that time. There have been many points in history since then when the "signs" of the end of times were all present and the end did not occur. Many contradictions in the Biblical text cannot be explained. I am very selective in my use of the Bible for that reason. The revelations of today have much more to say to me than the Bible. Most Bible study groups echo the theistic concept of God, a god that can be angered, vindictive and displeased. It would be refreshing to find one that includes current Biblical scholarship and not the theistic cultural story.

The Koran (Qur'an) is the revered text of the Islam community. The *Quran* meaning "the recitation"; (also Romanized *Qur'an*)**.** The *Koran* is the central religious text of Islam, which Muslims believe to be a revelation from God (Allah). Its origin is about 650 CE.

The *Book of Mormon* is the guiding text for the Mormon faith tradition; it is even more recent in human history. These two and many other older sacred texts each have a kernel of divine truth, but struggle to describe a God of unconditional love - love without judgment, vengeance or punishment. There are always religious dictates that describe how we should live and they don't all agree on how God wants us to worship or what God really wants from us.

I could site other sacred texts and their inconsistencies, but these examples illustrate a problem of being tied to just one "book" as the ultimate guide to eternal life. That problem is tribal religion and the tribal book.

Tribal Religion: Religious structures all have some kind of hierarchy that insures uniformity of belief, a system of beliefs ensconced in various creeds, doctrines and dogmas, which clearly state that religion's truths. To ensure its future, anointed members of that faith tradition are appointed to interpret these truths through religious services and schools to the members of that faith community. The tribe has a leader and teacher – an imam, priest, minister, rabbi or shaman. The congregations are the tribal members who depend upon the tribal leader for their understanding and interpretation of that faith tradition and truths. Once this is established, they live in the security of their truths and feel the need to protect them. A wall has been built around these beliefs and any other faith tradition is looked upon as suspect and as a threat. History tells us the rest of the story of aggression and killing all in the name of a loving god backed by their understanding of the truth. Many wars have stemmed from this. If our sacred text shows times when god hated the enemies that the believing community hated, then it is our obligation to defend the truth. The Old Testament is filled with numerous examples of god's people defeating their enemies. This defeat was clearly god's will and his might was with them. When the fences we build are threatened, hostilities result. This is true of religions, states, territories, nations and businesses protecting their assets. It is an ancient way of thinking that has not served us well at times. Tribal thinking gets in the way of unity, cooperation and our true reason for being here.

In situations like these, people defer to the tribe leader for interpretation and wisdom. They give away their power to a leader. They do not exercise critical thinking of their own. They are indoctrinated in "groupthink" or ideas that reinforce the beliefs of the group. They would rather follow the "rules" than think for themselves.

John Shelby Spong in responding to a question from one having doubts about the Bible gave this response:

> *Your problem is rather that in all your years as an Anglican, you were never educated by the church you attended. You were instead propagandized by biblical nonsense masquerading as Christian Education. No reputable biblical scholar in the last 200 plus years has treated many of the stories in the Bible as if they were literally true.*[2]

So, it would seem we have some things to "unlearn" from our past: how and where do we do that? We can start by looking beyond the fence lines or walls of our sacred text.

Sacred Texts for today: Trying to wrestle with divine revelation that is 2000 years old also begs the question, "Does God communicate with us today?" The answer is "Yes." God has spoken throughout all the ages if we chose to listen and look beyond the boundaries of our sacred texts. I have found three sacred texts that contain no contradictions, one ancient and two recent, whose teachings are based on a God of unconditional love. They prescribe no norms for worship.

One was written 500 years before Jesus walked the planet. It is the **Tao Te Ching** by Lau Tsu. It is a classic work concentrating on developing an inclusive non-judgmental spiritual outlook. Wayne Dyer spent a year studying this work and offers the following description from his book, *Change Your Thoughts – Change Your Mind:*

> *Many scholars consider this Chinese classic the ultimate discourse on the nature of existence; and it continues to be a valuable resource for achieving a way of life that guarantees integrity, joy, peace and balance.[3]*

The Tao refers to the supreme reality, an all-prevailing source of everything. The Tao is the loving force of the universe. The book avoids naming this reality, but says that it is the Source of all that is. The Tao is referred to as the Way. It has been translated more than any volume in the world with the exception of the Bible. It is a very enlightened work considering how early in our history it was written. It is amazing that the text survived the centuries since its inception. God in this work is described not as a person, but as the loving, life giving force of All That Is (another name for God).

More recently, in the 1970s, *A Course in Miracles* was given to the people of our time. It was given to Helen Schucman who scribed the book over a three-year period. Helen said that she understood the source as the voice of Jesus. In reading this work, the author sometimes speaks in the first person, from the perspective of Jesus in clarifying or correcting an interpretation of a Bible passage. The focus of this work centers on being in charge and in control of thoughts. At any moment in time, we can choose differently about what thoughts occupy our minds. We may not be able to control all the thoughts that enter our mind, but we can determine how long they stay there and what we do with them.

The Course is composed of a 669 page text explaining the concept of miracles; a 488 page Workbook for Students which contains 365 daily lessons; a 92 page Manual for Teachers which includes a text called *A Clarification of Terms*. There are also two supplements: *Psychotherapy and The Song of Prayer*.

Robert Holden, author of *Holy Shift*, has been a student of the Course for a long time and offers some additional comments:

> *Although the Course is written in Christian language, it is studied by my friends who are Buddhist, Muslim and Jewish because it offers a spiritual philosophy that reflects perennial wisdom.*
>
> *The Course describes a miracle as something you experience when you are*

> willing to shift your perception from a psychology of fear to a psychology of love.
>
> The Course teaches that forgiveness is more than just positive thinking, an emotional reframe, or the overlooking or forgetting of a specific event. Forgiveness is a spiritual path, according to the Course. It is the holy purpose of our life on earth. "Forgiveness is the home of miracles," says the Course. Through forgiveness, we remember who we are.[4]

Barbara and I have studied the Course for more than ten years and it has been a reliable guide to inner peace and changing the way we see people and the world we live in.

The third work is called *A Course of Love*. Mari Perron in the late 90's wrote what was given her over a period of several years. Like Helen Schucman, she took great pains to ensure the integrity of the work. It has a Text, Treatises, The Dialogues and a 40-Day meditation. The two books, *A Course in Miracles* and *A Course of Love* complement each other. *The Course in Miracles* works with thought discipline - training the mind in love vs. fear. *A Course of Love* teaches us to live from the feelings of the heart with the mind and heart in harmony. *A Course of Love* clearly states that it is a companion book to *A Course in Miracles*. Both, I believe, are divine revelations for us in our time and are very Christ centered.

The mind is what analyzes the world we live in; the heart is where we live with our feelings and emotions. It is the heart that we need to listen to. Gregg Braden echoes this theme in his writings. The heart will tell us the truth if we can listen. The key is to bring the mind and heart in agreement to where the two are one. Thus, do both books have a role to play in spiritual formation?

These recent revelations and texts have one thing in common – They are blueprints for developing a genuine spirituality based on personal development and the advancement of the soul, the person and a relationship with a God of unconditional love. Members of any faith tradition can use this approach because the approach is an individual, personal, spiritual development and growth.

The interesting thing about all three of the texts referenced here is that none of them encourage or hint of building a religion around them. In fact, *A Course in Miracles* specifically discourages that. These are for personal spiritual formation meant for individuals who are ready for this material. They likely will not enjoy the popularity of many sacred texts, but are pearls of great price for those who are called to them.

Theology vs. a God Experience: Now imagine that you are at another of your regular Sunday church services. Instead of the second reading, a five-minute personal testimony is given by a Muslim woman of her experience of God in her life, and doing so without quoting anything from the Koran. Then the minister enters the podium and ties it all together for the congregation. It is the experience of God that is our common language, not theology or quotes from a sacred text. Her testimony was not meant to challenge or argue any theological point. It is simply meant to talk about how she has experienced God in her life. Again, God is God and God is Love wherever we find that reality. On this same day, a member of your congregation is visiting their Mosque to share one "experience" of God working in his/her life while not quoting anything from the Bible. *A Course in Miracles* makes a clear statement about this:

> *Theological considerations, as such, are necessarily controversial, since they depend on belief and can therefore be accepted or rejected. A universal theology is impossible, but a universal experience is not only possible, but necessary. It is the experience toward which the Course is directed. Here alone, consistency becomes possible because, here alone, uncertainty ends.*[4]

So often we end up arguing theological issues when we should be concentrating on our experiences of the Divine at work in all our lives. I love to use this approach when door-to-door missionaries want to quote Bible passages to me, I usually ask them, "How is the Lord at work in your lives?" – and focus on our common experience rather than controversial theology or arguing the value of one sacred text versus another. I am ready to share how God is present in my life.

Summary: This chapter addresses religious adherence and allegiance to the sacred text of a faith tradition. Many of these texts are centuries old. In almost all cases, they are laced with a god of conditional love, one of reward and punishment. Religious people often let their congregational leader do their thinking for them. Instead of examining what they believe, they want to be told what to believe. The new spirituality tells us that we do not need some external authority to tell us what to believe and what is real.

Ram Dass, a spiritual teacher puts it this way:

> *I've finally come to the conclusion that there are no 'thems' for me anymore. I can't be told who to hate, who to fight, whom to subdue. I only see an 'us' in my heart.*[4]

We need to see that we are all connected in the Godlike collective called the 'Sonship' and work to eliminate barriers to love in our outlooks. Moving from a spirituality of fear to one of love is the goal of any valid spiritual path and the lifetime goal for all of us. So the bottom line is not to be tied exclusively to the tenets of a "book" for spiritual guidance, but trust yourself that you will discover a meaningful and dynamic spirituality. Yes, you can do it!

With all the confusing ideas presented to us to sort through, it is important to be able to separate the false from the true. The next chapter offers some simple tools anyone can use to discover where the Holy Spirit is at work.

[1] From the Weekly Question and Answer Blog by John Shelby Spong, October 2014
[2] Change Your Thoughts-Change Your Mind, by Wayne Dyer, (c. 2007), Preface p. xi
[3] Holy Shift, by Robert Holden, (c. 2014), Introduction, p. xii
[4] A Course in Miracles, (c. 1977), Introduction p. 215
[5] Inspiration, by Wayne Dyer, (c. 2006), p.220. Attributed to a lecture given by Ram Dass, a spiritual teacher and author

Developing a Good Crap Detector

*Just as we must always have faith,
we must always question our creeds
and make sure that our beliefs
bring us closer to God and the truth.*
-Bishop Desmond Tutu

I remember reading an interview that a journalist did with Ernest Hemmingway. He was trying to get to the basic idea of what makes a good writer. After asking several questions and getting a "no" answer from Hemmingway, he finally just asked what it took to be a good writer. Hemmingway's answer was simple: "To be a good writer, you need to have a functioning on-board crap detector." That simple statement says volumes.

I recall talking with my dad about the time the Second Vatican Council happened. There were changes in the liturgy of the church. He was not sure why the changes were necessary and expressed some confusion about them. I realized that he didn't have the background to evaluate why the changes were necessary and had been comfortable with the way things were. I, on the other hand, was still in the seminary. I anticipated the new changes as the "fresh air" that was needed in the church to relate more meaningfully to the times we lived in. The priests of that time did their best to explain the reason behind the changes and eventually, people settled into the new way of doing things.

It is often difficult to sort out what is real and meaningful in the religious realm and what is not. But there are some simple guidelines that will help sort things out. It is important to recognize which changes, sermons and congregational culture are of the Holy Spirit and which are definitely not.

The Holy Spirit is "inclusive": This is the first guideline: Love does not exclude or draw lines as to who is "in" and who is "out." Historically, the creeds of the church were used to determine who were saved and who were not. I recall visiting with a young woman in her early twenties who knew she was a lesbian. She not only felt her faith congregation did not accept her into the fold but saw her as not acceptable in the eyes of the Lord, or their lord anyway. She had looked around but had not found a faith community where she could feel accepted and safe. I knew there were congregations in the community that welcomed gays and lesbians and assured her that the Spirit was at work there for the Holy Spirit never "excludes" anyone. I encouraged her to continue to search for a community she could call home.

The gay/lesbian issue is a hot button for churches today. Good friends of mine, who are straight, used this rule in looking for a new faith community to join – whether the church accepted gays and lesbians or not. They wanted to be part of an inclusive congregation. Regardless of what Leviticus 20 says, gays and lesbians are precious sons and daughters of our Creator and those congregations that understand this and accept all, reveal the fingerprints of the Holy Spirit at work.

The way the Catholic Church treated divorced members, made of them like second-class citizens and not unconditionally accepted into the church community. In most cases, they were denied access to the Sacraments.

Priests who left the fold were excommunicated and sometimes there was a letter to back this up from Rome. Excommunication was always a big threat if one did not buy into the party line of the Church.

Suicide was another way of excluding. It was believed that if a person committed suicide, that person was guilty of serious sin and would not go to heaven and would not receive a Christian burial. The Church would not condone that action. It was believed that those who committed suicide went to hell.

Serious sin also excluded a person's access to the Sacraments until dealt with in the Sacrament of Penance. That was the only sacrament available to a person in that situation with the exception of the Sacrament of the Sick which also forgives serious sin near end of life.

One True Church and Chosen People: Growing up, I was taught that there was no salvation outside the Catholic Church. It was the one true Church founded by Jesus through Peter. This should be a red flag for anyone looking for a faith community in which to grow. No one faith tradition has all the answers and the exclusive truth to guide us "home." If a church says "our way is the only way" run as fast as you can. There is no One True Church. This is an example of being exclusive rather than inclusive. For some faith traditions, there is usually a penalty for leaving such a community – that is you will not be numbered among the saved. It is good to remind us that all religions are man-made institutions based around a set of beliefs of a spiritual leader. When that leader died, the teachings were codified into a sacred text and often modified over the centuries.

Look for communities where you can feel the love and thus the hand of God at work therein, e.g. congregations that do not put down or criticize other faith traditions so that they can feel superior. There should be no penalties for leaving any faith community for any reason. The Holy Spirit penalizes no one ever. There is a false sense of security and superiority in being a member of the chosen people enjoying god's favor and blessings versus those who were not.

I recall another hospital visit where a family was visiting their teenaged child. They were just thrilled that he decided to accept Jesus as his personal savior and that now he was numbered among the "saved." I could sense their relief that he was now inside the fold and not on the outside looking in. They had an inner peace knowing that salvation was theirs and now their son would someday be with them in heaven. That perspective is based on the belief that god shows favoritism and that his flock is special. We are not special but part of the mass of humanity (we are all chosen) that is plodding along like everyone else to find answers to life's questions. *The Course in Miracles* states that in God's sight, *"All of us are special; none of us is (more) special."*[1] God loves us all equally. Their son did not need to be saved; God loved him as much as those who were already "saved." They could have saved themselves some worry.

Theistic alert, the home of guilt and fear: The theistic god is still around at least in peoples' minds. My crap detector is quick to pick this up whenever I encounter it either in worship services, sermons, or conversations. This needn't be complicated. Whenever you sense any of the following, you know that you are witnessing a re-broadcast of the old order, the cultural story of the theistic god.

God can be offended or angered: We can displease god. This reflects the god of conditional love. This god looks suspiciously like parent figures we see here on Earth. The Old Testament is filled with examples of god becoming angry with his chosen people because they were not keeping the "divine directives." These accounts just reflect a primitive understanding of who god is as they understood it. Later understandings reflected a more expansive concept that God cannot be moved to anger, punishment and vengeance because there is no offense taken nor is there anger in unconditional love. God has nothing to do with "evil" in the world. He does not sponsor it, recognize it or account for it. The Prodigal Son parable is a good example of this. Read it and ponder its truth. But what of all the other references in the Bible that say otherwise? Yes, I know they are there, but again, it all stems from the author's understanding of who God is. The New Testament reflects what the Christians of the first century thought and experienced after Jesus died. They thought (and some still think) that god is going to come in and "fix" everything and set things straight, that he does not approve of sin and evil. If there is one attribute about God, it is that God is extremely patient and waits for us to finally figure it out and get it right. In a real sense, He is waiting for us to fix our situation. We should be the answer to our own prayers for peace and harmony. So I listen for hints asking god to fix our world. Often the prayers of the faithful at the Catholic Mass reflect a lot of this thinking.

Jesus died for my sins: This is an often repeated theme in liturgies. This comes from a misguided theology that because of the fall from god's grace in the Garden of Eden, we are of a fallen and imperfect nature. It is the old cultural story we grew up with. We are sinful and in need of redemption. Because we were incapable of redeeming ourselves, god sent his only begotten son (a divine member of the Trinity) to take on flesh and blood and through his death on the cross- redeemed mankind. Only a divine representative could make reparation for the sin of Adam. That thinking has endured for centuries, not because it was true, but because of the belief in a god who had punished Adam and his descendants for disobeying his command. In reading any of the accounts of Jesus' passion and death, it becomes clear that his death was the result of his constantly challenging the established hierarchy and practices of the Jewish religion at that time. They felt threatened and had had enough. Jesus was the "heresy" in their midst and had to be dealt with. Are there not numerous examples in history where this has happened over and over again – where people die because of a difference of opinion? Jesus' message of love challenged some hypocrisies of his time and he lovingly paid a price for it. Maybe when we read the passion and death accounts we should put our religion and ourselves in Jesus' shoes and see how we all stack up!

God will love you if you follow his commandments: This phrase is often heard in sermons and worship services. Again, this needs little commentary. St. Paul says that there is nothing that can keep us from God's love. When we are made to feel like miserable sinners in need of divine mercy, alarms should be sounded. We are precious children in His sight and like the prodigal son, totally accepted.

You should live in the "fear of the lord:" I think this reflects a normal human reaction to being in the presence of an all-powerful entity and a feeling that such power could be used against us. But there is a more correct understanding and a way to say what this phrase is trying to instruct us – that we need to respect and praise such an entity. Perhaps the more accurate way to put this is that we should be in "awe" in the presence of God. Awe does not carry the connotation of fear, but more of our acknowledgment and wonderment. There is no fear in unconditional love.

When the main theme is one of "Lord have mercy on me" or that we are unworthy: We are always worthy and welcomed to be in God's presence because we are His children.

When your experience is not a joyful one: If your experience in a faith community is not infused with joy, then analyze what your experience is about. Joy is one of the fruits or signs of the Holy Spirit.

When you are made to feel like you need to go out and spread the good news and bring others into the fold: When you feel like your church has been given the blueprint or the way back to Home, members feel they have to get that word out to the world. God does not want martyrs or missionaries. He only wants us to live our lives so that the light that we are shines out for the world to see.

When Jesus is elevated as the only begotten Son of the Father: Jesus is a very enlightened soul; our brother has God-like qualities just like we do. He is part of the vast Sonship as are we.

When gays and lesbians are put down, discredited or not accepted: This is a blatant sign that does not exhibit the presence of God. God does not exclude.

When the Ten Commandments are stressed over the New Testament command that Jesus brought us: Jesus didn't bring us ten more rules to follow, but challenged us to figure out what "to love" means. Following the rules won't buy us salvation. We are New Testament people.

When what we do in this lifetime will determine heaven or hell for all eternity: St. Peter at his station outside the Pearly Gates was an invention of someone's mind. Hell is also an invention of mankind and for centuries was used to keep the faithful in line. God gives us many opportunities to get it right-other lifetimes.

There is no salvation outside of the church: Salvation is not limited to one faith tradition. There are many paths to God.

These are some of the tenets of the theistic concept of god that should get your attention and realize that they are talking about a god that never really existed. The only places where this god existed were in the minds of those who believed in this illusion.

Once you accept the God of unconditional love as the **God Who IS** and always was and always will be, then the god of conditional love stands out like a sore thumb, easy to recognize and identify.

Does it all depend on this one lifetime? Many homilies seem to imply that the lifetime we are living is the only chance we get for salvation. To add to that, at the end of this "one lifetime," a judgment will be made by god that will have eternal consequences. There is much evidence that we live and have lived multiple lifetimes. "Then how come we don't know about the other lives we've led?" you could ask. These have sometimes been revealed and verified through hypnosis and past life regressions. Frankly, it would be a distraction if we were aware of those past lives during our time here. We will know all about them when it is time to lay our bodies aside and return Home.

Judgment and observation: This is a fine but important line to draw; knowing the difference can enhance our earthly life and advance our spiritual life. The following example might illustrate the difference: A co-worker didn't do what they said they would do. **Observation:** the job didn't get done. **Judgment:** the job didn't get done *because* he thought another task was more important or because he was lazy or disorganized. Attaching a reason to the observation makes it a judgmental statement.

Gary Zukav in his book, The *Seat of the Soul*, provides additional insights about this issue:

> *There are personalities that are selfish, hostile and negative, but even in these cases we cannot fully know the reasons why. These are hidden from view. That does not mean that we cannot recognize negativity when we see it, but we cannot judge it. That is not our place. If we can intervene in an argument, or break up a fight, it is not appropriate that we judge the participants. Of one thing we can be certain: a person that is engaging in violence is hurting deeply, because a healthy and balanced soul is incapable of harming another.*[2]

This is a valuable skill to develop because in listening to others, you can see if they are making an observation or being judgmental about a situation or person and apply the same to yourself. We get in trouble most of the time because of the judgments we make whether spoken or thought. It cuts a lot of crap out of your life if your detector is working properly.

Fear vs. Love: All decisions are based on either love or fear. Emotions can be categorized in the same way. Our goals for each incarnation are to change from making decisions based on fear and security and to make decisions based on love. The illusions of this world are filled with fear. If you are in a position of authority in your job, there are challenges that often put you on the defensive. Whenever you make decisions that are pulling back and defensive, those are based on fear. A lot of decisions nationally are fear-based bent on protecting and keeping us safe. Military expansion is all fear-based. Getting a home security system is a fear-based decision. Not getting involved in issues is another example. After a while, we get better at seeing when we are acting out of fear or love.

I remember passing up people who were looking for a handout at stores or at stop signs. I did so because I felt they were likely to misuse that money and spend it on liquor. That was a fear-based decision and also a judgmental one. Now I just give them something and figure how they end up using it is their business. Someone once said, "they can make several hundred dollars a day doing that." So I say, "Let them." It is none of my business. It is that individual's business as to what is done with the money. If they are using that money to further an addiction or something that doesn't advance their lives, so be it. It is a relief to not have to be concerned with what they do. Getting rid of fear-based thoughts and decisions eliminates a lot of crap from one's spiritual journey.

Politics and Religion: If there ever was a dangerous marriage, it is when politics and religion get mixed together and confused. It is a perfect combination and not for the better. This is where a good "crap detector" is invaluable. When it comes to science, everything is verifiable and proof can be demonstrated. When it comes to politics and religion, we believe something because someone said so and we take that as proof that it is true. Perhaps it was someone in a position of authority, a top government official or leader of a religious group: a minister, priest, rabbi, imam or shaman. We tend to believe what they say because we feel they know more about the issue than we do or at least they are supposed to. We can use the same rule for religion as well as politics. Is what they are saying inclusive or are there groups that are excluded? Is what we hear coming from fear or love? Is what is being proposed going to advance civilization or a religious community? This is where a person uses all the tools in their detection toolbox in thinking for themselves.

When people hear a sermon or a speech, they may question what is being said. That is a good sign that they are thinking for themselves. This is a requirement in today's world. This is where the individual decides to be a part of the "group-think" message or not. It surely is easier to go along with the crowd than to try to swim upstream counter to what the group thinks. Just because someone says it is so doesn't mean that it really is so. Politicians sometimes lie outright and because they have channels of mass communication available to them. People usually don't question what they say. But that is exactly what should be done. The same goes for religion. Just because a religious leader talks about god in theistic terms doesn't mean that God really punishes and condemns. The biggest red flag for all of us should be when national proposals are couched in religious terms or when leaders pushing religious agendas wrap themselves in the national flag and the cross. In the end, the issue often isn't what is right or wrong, but is what we are doing working for all of us? If it works for the betterment of and advancement of, the human family should be the norm we use. Leaders have known for some time now that fear works to get people to follow them.

The quote from Herman Goering, Hitler's #1 propaganda man is an example for motivating people to follow their leader.

> *Why of course, people don't want war. But after all it is the leaders of the country that determine policy. And it's always a simple matter to drag the people along, whether it's a democracy, a fascist state...the people can always be brought to the bidding of the leaders. This is easy! All you have to do is tell them they are being attacked and denounce the pacifists for lack of patriotism and exposing the country to danger. It works the same in any country.[3]*

People may not know if any of what was said is true or not, but they will follow out of fear.

Then there is the issue of nationalism. Taking pride in one's country is usually a good thing, but can quickly become a restrictive thing when challenged. For example, ISIS set out to establish a Muslim Caliphate, or a religious state. Those who did not think like the leaders were ostracized or killed. The goal was that members of the Caliphate would be of like mind. If one's idea of governing is to kill off the opposition or those who don't agree with you, then you have a problem. We don't live in a homogenous world where everyone thinks along the same lines. Does a healthy society welcome diversity and see strength in diversity? Nationalism can be very exclusive if taken to extremes where it shouts defensiveness instead of pride.

Religions sometimes fare no better. Creeds were often used as a test to determine who was welcomed into the faith community and who was not. That is one reason why separation of church and state has always been a good idea. Combining the two can be devastating. We are seeing that in today's politics. A questioning mind will be able to see through the illusions that are out there. When people blindly follow a leader, they are giving up their power to that leader. Thinking for one's self is exercising our God given power and voice.

There is a lot of new thought about spirituality available today. Much of it we were never exposed to in our religious education, but having an idea of what our souls want needs to be explored. This is an understanding of the Psychology of the Soul and expands our understanding of our context here on earth and of ourselves.

Next are some concepts that may make life easier to understand.

[1] A Course in Miracles, Text 15 V 5:1
[2] The Seat of the Soul, by Gary Zukav, (c. 1989). P. 43 From Taped Lecture by Wayne Dyer in 2006. Quote is attributed to Herman Goring on propaganda and war.

Psychology of the Soul

The cycles of Life need to be approached with reverence.
They have been in place for billions of years.
- Gary Zukav

What we understand about our souls has come a long way for Christians since the original teachings of Jesus. But the good news is that this doesn't contradict the teachings of Jesus. It speaks of realities that the soul is about beyond this earthly incarnation. It is the study of Spiritual Psychology. Our souls are eternal. We do not die but continue on in spirit after death. The adventures of our souls are about so much more than what we experience or call this lifetime. This will be new territory for many, as the old cultural religious story doesn't address any of these at all. I doubt if the people of Jesus' time would have grasped the concepts if he had talked about them. Yet, there are several spiritual writers today describing a much more dynamic picture of the soul and the stages of life involved with incarnations.

When I began looking into this aspect of ourselves, it resonated with me that this is exactly how an all loving Creator would have designed it. It all made sense. A loving God would give us multiple opportunities to find our way Home. God is patient and He/She will wait until we figure it out – God's will for us is really also our will for us because God desires only what is best for us. This didn't fit with the concept of a god of "conditional" love. It only confirmed my belief that the Father, Creator, is unconditional love.

Multiple lifetimes: There is an overwhelming amount of evidence supporting this reality. Yes we all have lived multiple lifetimes and will likely live many more. People have done past life regressions and described events and places that they could only have known about if they had been there. So why are we not aware of those past lives? Frankly, I think it would be a distraction for what we are about in this lifetime. So it is a good thing. Past lives are a part of the progress we have made as souls to get to this one. All past lifetimes are a part of the planning that goes into this one. One temporal lifetime with eternal consequences doesn't seem to make sense.

This issue raised a lot of questions for me personally. In my ministry work, I witnessed babies who lived for only days or a couple weeks. I also attended the death of a 95-year-old man. If one lifetime, do or die, was the rule, what about the infant? They've done nothing wrong to deserve reward or punishment. Only multiple lifetimes seemed to answer this dilemma. I'll never know the reason for that short lifetime, because there is always more to what the soul is up to than we can see. This incarnation is but a small segment of the soul's long history of incarnations and adventures. That child may have come to help its parents learn a life lesson to deal with loss. Who knows for sure? But I am convinced that there is a reason for the child's short lifetime. That child's mission in this lifetime was completed. That child's soul may live a long and productive life with the next lifetime. So we do not see the big picture, the context in which our soul exists. Jesus is firm about the fact that we **cannot judge another** because we see only a segment of another soul's history. God and the Holy Spirit know our history and our goals for this lifetime. We can humbly ask our guides and the Holy Spirit for the guidance and wisdom to fulfill our life goals in our current life. When attending a death at the hospital, I often wonder if that person achieved the life lessons they set out prior to being born. Only God and that soul know for sure. Would not a loving God give his children all the chances to learn what it is they need to learn to evolve? Thus, the one lifetime, do or die for all eternity is out.

Again, there is so much more going on for each of us than what we see here. Therefore, it becomes difficult if not impossible to judge another's behavior or actions; we just don't see what they are all about.

Free Will: God does not interfere with our gift of free will. That is out of respect for us. We are free to make choices good or not so good. We are free to find out what it means to love. We are free to make mistakes and to make another decision to correct those mistakes. There is no mistake that cannot be forgiven by God. We may totally waste a lifetime by making horrible decisions. That is our choice. Our ability to choose is a precious gift endowed by our Creator. So we are free to decide what to feed our bodies and minds. Like earthly decisions where what we feed our bodies has consequences, fear based decisions also have consequences. Earthly parents give children multiple opportunities to learn life's lessons by allowing them to try something out to see what happens within reason. Our Father is patient with us. If we don't learn a life lesson this round, we can set it up to learn in the next lifetime or the next until we get it right. Our God is not a jealous god. God is a very patient God.

Universal Salvation: Does this mean that all of God's children will eventually be saved in the end? Does this also mean that no one will be lost or in hell for all eternity? The Bible presents a problem here when considering the last book of the New Testament, the Book of Revelation. It seems that Jesus returns indeed to separate the sheep from the goats to an eternal reward or punishment. I had a problem with that because why would Jesus' second coming be so different from his first when he walked among us? This also does not jive with the concept of a God of unconditional love. There are all kinds of judgments and conditions contained in the Book of Revelations. But then would an all-loving God ever leave one of his cherished children behind? So if we are all going to eventually complete all our incarnations and be at one with God in the end, is there really a place called hell? The concept of universal salvation has been a controversial one but is usually not a part of the narrative when talking about a god of conditional love. Hell for all eternity makes no sense in light of multiple lifetimes and all that happens between lifetimes. Hell was man's invention of trying to make sense out of all the injustice in the world that justice must be done and a price paid after this lifetime. My personal belief is that there is no place called hell, but we see to it ourselves that justice is done by what we do in other lifetimes.

What universal salvation means is that all those who are committing heinous crimes such as child molesters, rapists, murderers, thieves, abusers and terrorists will be saved. This includes members of other faith traditions such as Islamists, Hindus, Buddhists, Jews and devil worshippers. Does this list also include the Hitlers of the world? It includes every person who has ever lived, is here now and who will be. Again, we struggle to understand why God could love a Hitler. Why didn't god step in and correct things before six million people died in the process? Why does god permit evil to flourish? Could it be that God does not interfere with our free will or ability to choose and does so out of respect for us? Might that be an attribute of love without conditions?

Philip Gulley, a pastor, summarized the issue in the following quote from his book – *If Grace is True- God Will Save Every Person:*

> *When I tell of God's persistence, some are moved to tears. When I suggest that God's love, patience and persistence never end, many become angry. One woman said, "I've worked hard to live a good life, and now you tell me everyone is going to get in." I don't have much sympathy for such a response. Such self-righteousness offended Jesus, who spoke tenderly to sinners but reserved his harshest words for those who gloried in their own goodness.*[1]

The key here is that **eventually** everyone will be saved, but not until many lifetimes and many life lessons learned have been completed will that be a reality. Would an all-loving – all-patient God be any different? That is the role and purpose of multiple lifetimes.

Contracts / pre-incarnation agreements, helping each other to get home: This may seem far out, but see if it makes sense to you. This is a task that every soul takes very seriously. It is a relatively new concept to me that seems in line with an all-loving Creator. What are contracts about? These are agreements that each of us makes with other souls prior to an incarnation to facilitate our goals and the life lessons we've set out for that lifetime. It might be someone in our life that creates a problem that we have to deal with and learn from; e.g. a soul who incarnates as our brother with an addiction problem. We go to great lengths in planning a lifetime to work with other souls who will help us and possibly in turn, we help them. We are here to help each other to facilitate our life lessons and learnings.

It is surprising to many to learn that we do choose our parents and the families we are born into. This is not a random event. This is important because souls are looking for families that will provide an environment that will encourage them with their life lessons. That includes the tone the parents set as well as what the other siblings are about with their life lessons in that family. We also decide the gender, race, the day of our birth, country and cultural setting that will best serve our chosen life lessons.

Contracts and life planning can also include a business partner who steals from you or a child who dies prematurely – a life lesson of loss – or a marriage partner who files for divorce, etc. Contracts are sometimes short term. Just look at the people that have come and gone in your lifetime. Some fulfilled a purpose that posed a problem or helped you advance or realize greater awareness, etc. It might include a church you once belonged to, or a close friend that you no longer have contact with, or someone who provided an opportunity to advance in your education or career. These are examples of short-term contracts that have been completed. Others are long-term contracts such as a life-long marriage or business partner. This planning is extensive and we all have gone to great lengths to make primary and backup plans for the lifetimes we live. These incarnations are incredibly important opportunities for every soul to grow and evolve in its learning and wisdom. Every soul approaches every incarnation with extensive planning – enlisting the help of other souls who will incarnate during our lifetime.

Wayne Dyer – addresses this topic in the following excerpt:

> *On earth, we have been given the gift of volition (that is, we can choose), so let's assume that we had the same capacity when we resided in the spirit realm. We chose our physical body, just as we chose our parents we needed for the trip. And it doesn't seem*

too great a stretch to believe that we chose this life in concert with our Source (God).[2]

Some souls choose bodies with physical defects or mental problems for reasons that fulfill a goal of that chosen lifetime. It is not for us to figure out why that happened. That situation was carefully planned by that soul prior to incarnation. So there is a lot of effort that goes into planning the next incarnation. It happens between lifetimes. We often wonder how souls spend their time between lifetimes. Now we have a clue.

About birth and dying: Birth and death is really the same thing as both are times of transition. From the spirit world, we work with other kindred souls to get ready to be born. We have observed our future families and when all seems right we prepare for being born. Souls that assist us on the spirit side to get ready for birth are saddened when we leave the spirit world. Our soul has to lower its frequency to incarnate. Of the two transitions, birth is the most difficult for the incoming soul. Death is an easier transition as the soul's vibration rises back to its normal frequency of the spirit world. Just as people on this side of the veil mourn the loss of a soul that has transitioned to the spirit world, souls on the spirit side rejoice at the return of the soul to Home. So there are souls on both sides of the veil that assist with each transition.

People sometimes worry about someone dying alone. Of course, dying is a very individual act, but in a sense, we are never alone. Accounts of people close to dying may see someone they know who has come to assist them with their transition whereas others in the same room don't see anything. In planning a lifetime, we contract with someone to be our "greeter" or be there when we lay the body aside and transition Home. In working with the No One Dies Alone program at the hospital, our team understands that some people prefer to not have family around when they die while others do prefer that someone be present.

Life reviews: So we live a lifetime and then we die. After death, we get to do a "life review" of our most recent lifetime with the help of other souls. This is the first activity that we engage in when we return Home. In his book, *Five People You Meet in Heaven*, Mitch Albom describes what a life review is about. It is an objective, unemotional look at the life just lived realizing how you saw things as well as knowing how others were affected by what you did or didn't do. It is from this review that we come to realize if we achieved our goals for our recent lifetime or not. If not, then another lifetime or more will be needed and planned for. It is possible to waste a lifetime, or not achieve the goals set out for it. God is patient and will wait until we have lived enough lives to see the light and evolve in our understanding.

Gary Zukav describes this process:

> *Until you become aware of the effects of your anger, you will continue to be an angry person. If you do not reach this awareness by the time you return Home, your soul will continue this lesson through the experiences of another lifetime. It will incarnate another*

> *personality with aspects that are similar to your own. What is not learned in each lifetime is carried over into other lifetimes, along with new lessons that arise for the soul to learn. The lessons that the soul has learned are also brought forward into other lifetimes and this is how the soul evolves.*
>
> *Eventually, you will come to understand that love heals everything and love is all there is. This journey may take many lifetimes but you will complete it. It is impossible not to complete it. It is not a question of "if" but "when.[3]*

If all of this seems foreign, it just reminds us that there is always more to us than what we see in this lifetime. Is all this necessary to know about? It is probably not a requirement as many people live and die everyday without being aware of this, but I find it fascinating to think about and it is consistent with a God of unconditional love. This knowledge takes some of the terror out of the prospect of dying.

I had the privilege of talking with a gentleman in the hospital who was conscious and knew he was within days of dying. He said that he was not afraid. That opened the door for us to talk about what we thought about dying. I shared some ideas with him and asked him to contact me after he died to let me know if what I was saying had any merit. We both laughed, but it was a spirit lifting experience. His courage and inner peace were evident. Most of the people we attend to in the 'No One Dies Alone' program are comatose and not interactive, so I cherished the opportunity to visit with one who could talk openly about his impending death.

What people often experience after death is being surrounded and supported by an intelligent and loving presence regardless of the life we have just completed. It would seem then that there is no hell between lifetimes but a time of review and rest between incarnations. Again, judgment, vengeance, punishment and anger are not attributes of the God of unconditional love.

Recent information: This section of the book is open to discussion. You can take this with a grain or a pound of salt as you wish, but I pass this along for your consideration. I am inclined to believe what is being said about our current place in the history of the human race on Earth. Some people channel spirits or souls from the other side of the veil. These souls provide information to help us in our human evolution. The information coming from several sources is remarkably consistent and it warns of future events and directions the human race is headed. Regardless of what you think of channeled information, just consider the message and don't get distracted by how it was delivered.

The Message: These souls tell us that we are witnessing times like none other on the planet. These are not ordinary times and are unique and of importance in the history of mankind. Mankind is on the cusp of an historical event. If we look around and back during our lifetimes, we have witnessed events that have taken place in a short time with serious consequences. No generation before us has had to decide the issues we face today. Global warming is a reality and has generally been ignored by the powers that be. The poles are melting at a rapid rate and sea levels are expected to rise and threaten many coastal communities. The world population has watched and done little to change the way they live. The industrial revolution has put far too much greenhouse gases into the atmosphere and it is more than our mother earth can handle. Mankind has used the oceans as dumping grounds that has degraded them. Oceans are becoming more acidic and much marine life is threatened, especially barrier reefs and the life they support. Certain wildlife habitats are disappearing and that has implications for the food chain. Our weather has obviously changed. We have not worked in harmony with the Earth, our home, and what many consider our "mother" upon whom we are all dependent upon for safety and life support. As a result, we have set up a series of events that will have a serious impact on our earthly lives.

The most recent information is that the earth has passed a critical tipping point and is in decline. Science has determined the magnetic field that protects us from the harmful effects of the sun is weakening. We will become more vulnerable to solar flares and other solar radiation. The Earth is heading for a polar shift (which has happened several times throughout history). There is some concern that this one will be different. In the past life survived these shifts, which lasted a matter of days. There is some concern about this one. The timetable for all of this is said to be 50-80 years. The difference will be in how we respond to the current situation on the planet – how we care for mother earth. If we take action sooner than later, that time can be extended. The decisions we make on a daily basis will have consequences down the line. Unfortunately, big money has driven many of these decisions on national scales and let the damage continue so as to amass their fortunes. So consequences are on the horizon it seems. This is clearly not the world we grew up in.

To add to the excitement, we will witness political events like never before, some good and others not so good. It is no secret that half of the world's nations are at war and tension on the planet is at an all-time high. We all need to pay attention to what is going on in our country, state and community. We can have a voice in future outcomes assuming our vote still count. We have never seen political times like these either. There are forces at work that may exacerbate our situation. But these souls also tell us that there is some positive energy that is coming and will make a difference. We will see better times also. We'll all have to wait and see on that prediction.

Anyway, it will pay to be alert and informed. A good spiritual grounding will be important in facing the future, not one of fear, but of hope; one that is inclusive and not exclusive; one that sees all as our brothers and sisters dependent upon each other in a good way. Every decision we make is made out of either fear (which includes hate, anger, complaint and exclusion) or love. Love is the key to a good spiritual grounding. As time goes forward, take these words to heart and see if these predictions materialize.

It is time to take a look at organized religions of the world and what role they play in the big scheme of things. How will these survive when challenged with the new emerging spirituality?

---

[1] If Grace is True – God Will Save Every Person, by Philip Gulley and James Mulholland, (c. 2003), p. 161
[2] Inspiration, by Wayne Dyer, (c. 2006), p. 17
[3] The Seat of the Soul, by Gary Zukav, (c. 1989), p. 120

Do we need organized religion?

*We want to be people of faith,
not people drugged on the narcotic of religion.*
- John Shelby Spong

What is the role of organized religion? Does it serve a temporary purpose? Does it provide a basis to make our spiritual decisions? Is it compatible with contemporary thinking on spirituality? All of these questions have major implications.

It is no secret that the mainline churches, both Catholic and Protestant, are declining in membership and that religion is undergoing challenges in these times. Will they change or just die out? But before we prepare for the burial service, let's take a closer look at the positives and negatives of it all. How has Christianity served humanity to date? The church has had a positive as well as a negative influence. On the positive side, it carried civilization through the dark ages. It started the system of higher education, which has matured into what we have today. The church was responsible for building the first health care system or hospitals. The church emphasized the sacredness of life. It also fostered great music, architecture and art. These are tremendous accomplishments in themselves.

It is also no secret that Christianity has had a dark side. Throughout the ages religious persecution, wars and the Inquisition which was church orchestrated is no badge of honor. It often interpreted the Bible passages to justify societal ills such as slavery, subjugation of women and condemning homosexuality. It has pitted one religious tradition against another.

It seems that there are two sides to this, and one of them has a criminal history. In looking at the list of crimes, many persist today. In looking at the world situation, it can easily be seen that religion is the biggest obstacle to peace today.

Religious beliefs have been at the core of many conflicts around the world and throughout history. Why can't we all "just get along?" Apparently it is easier said than done. But I think it is fair to say that religion will have to change or face its demise through attrition. Whereas in the past it has served a purpose to bring humanity through some tough times, it struggles to rise above and address the issues that humanity faces today. Religion has rarely taken the lead in any positive social change throughout history and most often has assumed a defensive posture on change.

In looking at the world situation, Islam is under fire and defensive about anyone who criticizes their Prophet. They are out to punish the world for its irreverence. Certain practices within the Islam faith tradition, especially where women are concerned, seem hard to defend in a world that has instant communication worldwide and where people are less isolated. People know what is going on in other parts of the world. I believe Islam is the first of the major faith traditions that will face major reform or become irrelevant. When the women of Islam decide that it will be different, that will be the force of change.

Before Christians become too complacent, our time is coming. Maybe Christian churches don't have gross mistreatment of women, but there are issues that challenge the belief systems to the core. These have and will cause more division if the church's posture is defensive. It could also be the cause to re-examine our beliefs for a more open and inclusive position, which is more likely to bode well against a pattern of demise. The LGBTQ issue, same sex marriage, and systemic issues such as racism, poverty and human rights issues continue to challenge our current beliefs. So Christian churches are not immune nor will they escape the scrutiny that is sure to come.

The Hindu faith in India has had conflicts and issues with other religious sects there. The protestant-catholic conflict in Ireland and others all document unaddressed social injustices. It is often oppression in the name of organized religion. There is no need to list any more examples, as the world knows about them.

Religion vs Spirituality: A common expression people often use today is, "I am spiritual and not religious." In a nutshell, that statement says that a person belongs to no established or organized religious community, but is on a spiritual quest of their own. Some find the presence of God being in nature. Some are reading books on the new spirituality. Each has found a way to find some spiritual meaning which is their truth. I believe the Holy Spirit works with anyone who wants direction in their search. All they have to do is ask for it. Retired Bishop John Shelby Spong portrays these individuals as belonging to "the church alumni association." They once belonged but have graduated is the implication.

Now I have to say that I value the basic catholic school education, theological study and ministry experiences I've had. These are all part of a spiritual grounding from which I could base decisions and future directions for my own spirituality. So I think when parents want their children to have some religious education to start with, that is a good thing. Then as they get older, the children can decide if they want to stay with the faith of their upbringing or not. At least they have a starting point they can evaluate and decide upon their direction. In this role, it serves as a temporary service in a person's spiritual formation. People value the community and social aspects of the church and the connections and friendships they have developed there, are important. I don't want to underestimate what that can mean to people. Many will live out their entire lives within a congregation. It is comfortable to be with people who think like they do and they feel connected to that community. Religion has provided a comfort that serves them well. It is a secure environment; they feel at home.

The goal of religion is not to seek truth, but to provide security. If it were truth, faith communities would entertain and welcome questions about why they believe what they do. Like Jesus in his time, a viable religious community would challenge itself to examine creeds and doctrines and challenge those that no longer make sense or invite a person to greater spiritual heights.

Churches will often tell you their way is the only way to salvation and promise the security of knowing that you are saved. Don't believe it! There are many valid ways to achieve a viable spirituality. I wish all churches would preach this simple message that Neale Donald Walsch put forth in one of his books: *"Ours is one way; Ours is not a better way."*[1] If this were proclaimed from church pulpits throughout the world, wouldn't we be less quick to judge anyone else's spiritual path? I present these thoughts not to be emulated by anyone, but to get some insight into one man's search for meaning and faith. This is my story and quest for truth.

What does organized religion teach? When you look at what organized religions teach, these subjects come to mind: separation, need, superiority, failure, judgment and condemnation. So how is this taught?

Separation- the earth is our temporary home. We were separated from god through mankind's fall in the Garden of Eden. We are even separated from each other; we are individuals.

Need – we are desperately in need of redemption, of salvation. We are in need of god's mercy and forgiveness.

Superiority – We are the one True Church. We have the truth and others don't. We know what is right and wrong.

Failure – we have sinned. Ours is a fallen nature. We are not perfect. We have failed to meet the Gospel standards.

Judgment and Condemnation - we can judge the non-believers, other faith traditions, cultural morals and practices.

Please keep in mind that all religions are man-made institutions. Denominations and their political structure are limiting. Services are so predictable; the same-old-same-old Sunday after Sunday. Part of that is because the hierarchy of that religion has established some norms for conformity throughout its congregations. Congregations can't be self-directing or the diversity of worship would be all over the board. Even changing a simple response such as "The Lord be with you," to "Namaste" would take a lot of discussion before ordering the change. When translated, Namaste means **I honor the** Divine spark within each of us that is located in the **heart**. It is a greeting. The gesture is an acknowledgment of the soul in one by the soul in another, or I honor the Divine presence in you. A congregation could be called on the carpet for this change, and for sure, introducing readings from other faith traditions would never gain approval. This is just one of the issues that organized religion faces. Here is where "non-denominational" churches have an advantage – no hierarchy looking over their shoulders.

Did Jesus intend to found a church: The Roman Catholic Church has developed a tradition from scripture that traces the origins of the Church all the way back to St. Peter. In examining the teachings of Jesus, I wonder if He ever intended to found a religion organized around a set of beliefs or creeds that developed over time into a political structure with its hierarchy. The whole story of his passion and death narrative in scripture shows that he challenged the organized religious structure of his time constantly leading to his crucifixion and death. Haven't we seen that repeated numerous times throughout religious history?

Buddha was of a similar mind admonishing his followers not to make a religion out of his teachings, but they did anyway.

A Course in Miracles, a sacred text for today, strongly discourages putting its teachings into creeds, doctrines and forming religious groups. It stresses that it is an individualized course of study under the direction of the Holy Spirit. I feel that Jesus speaks through this text to us today and that is what makes me wonder if his intention ever was to found a "church."

Those who decide to leave the fold: Maybe the goal of organized religion is to graduate from it. In the 1960's and 70's, priests were leaving the fold of the Roman Catholic Church it seemed in droves. I have read letters from priests who have decided to leave the active ministry and they all have the common theme that the institutional Church is at odds with the "calling" they received. So, for me, the Catholic Church provided a framework, which I grew up with and eventually out of. It served a purpose and I am grateful for it. It was a stepping-stone to another level of awareness and not a set of beliefs I would be locked into for the rest of my life. Here is some testimony from two individuals who have left the fold.

James Kavanaugh in his book *God Lives*, describes his announcement to leave the Catholic Church, again finding more honesty outside the church structure than within it:

> *It happened as I talked to the students about the Church. I described its narrowness, its injustice, its superficial changes, and its lack of genuine contact with people. I saw the honest openness of the young faces about me. I had already told myself deep inside that I could no longer be a priest, and as I talked, I knew I had to tell the students. So I told them - in sudden and unexpected tears. Without shame, I told the Catholic Church with its abuse and distrust of people, and its cruel laws, as I knew them, to "go to hell." The auditorium was deathly silent for several seconds until students, nuns and even priests were on their feet shouting their long repressed approval. My priesthood was over.*[2]

Jimmy Carter's decision to sever ties with the Southern Baptist Convention was a significant event and came after much prayerful thought:

> *My decision to sever my ties with the Southern Baptist Convention, after six decades, was painful and difficult. It was, however, an unavoidable decision when the convention's leaders, quoting a few carefully*

selected Bible verses and claiming that Eve was created second to Adam and was responsible for original sin, ordained that women must be "subservient" to their husbands and prohibited from serving as deacons, pastors or chaplains in the military service.

At its most repugnant, the belief that women must be subjugated to the wishes of men excuses slavery, violence, forced prostitution, genital mutilation and national laws that omit rape as a crime. But it also costs many millions of girls and women control over their own bodies and lives, and continues to deny them fair access to education, health, employment and influence within their own communities. The impact of these religious beliefs touches every aspect of our lives.

The truth is that male religious leaders have had - and still have - an option to interpret holy teachings either to exalt or subjugate women. This is in clear violation not just of the Universal Declaration of Human Rights but also the teachings of Jesus Christ, the Apostle Paul, Moses and the prophets, Muhammad, and founders of other great religions - all of whom have called for proper and equitable treatment of all the children of God. It is time we had the courage to challenge these views.[3]

These are a couple examples of those who have decided to take a personal stand, to think for themselves about how beliefs impact the lives they lead and those impacted by those beliefs.

My own decision to leave the priesthood involved theological differences. I had some problems with the "party-line" of the Church. Celibacy I questioned. I felt that I might want someday to marry. Excluding women from ordination to the priesthood didn't seem right. Religious orders of Sisters were the closest women could come in ministry – not to full ordination to the priesthood. It made no sense to require people to attend Mass under penalty of sin. I felt the sacrament of penance was unnecessary and the doctrine of "sin" was a control issue. The Church's position on divorce punished those who were divorced. The process of getting a marriage annulled was cumbersome and took forever, it seemed. Then there was the cost of the annulment that had to be paid before a decision could be rendered. Divorcees were not members in full standing in the Church community. They were treated like second-class citizens. The issue of clerical status and privilege concerned me. It set me apart from the people as being part of the hierarchy.

These are just some of the issues as a priest, I felt pressured to profess and uphold because it was the policy of the Church organization.

Traditional Christianity and the emerging spirituality: Now for the big question: Is the new spirituality compatible with the traditional organized religion? The short answer, I am not sure that it is.

When considering multiple lifetimes, the evolution of the soul and the new revelations coming to us in our time, the language is surely different. These concepts are not talked about in the context of the Bible or in most of the traditional thinking of the past. It is hard to find a Bible verse that addresses multiple lifetimes, the Sonship or pre-life planning. The new vision hardly relates too much of my religious upbringing.

Then there's the issue of texts for spiritual guidance. The Bible is a book not free of contradictions. There are definitely parts of the Bible that I have difficulty even saying that, "This is the Word of the Lord." This is not to say that the Bible doesn't contain sacred truths – it sure does, but it is not to be taken literally. It is not an historical record.

I consider *A Course in Miracles* and *A Course of Love* to be both the voice of Jesus with wisdom and direction for our time. These texts are fresh and haven't been altered by anyone retranslating or changing the original text. Interestingly enough, this new revelation is very Jesus centered. Jesus did not get lost in the transition. Gary Renard characterizes *A Course in Miracles* as "Jesus without religion." The scribes of these texts both said they recognized that it was Jesus that spoke to them and was the author of them. They merely scribed what was given them. It all makes more sense to me now than it ever did. The new spirituality all fits together in a non-judgmental, non-contradictory manner that to me reflects perfectly a God of unconditional love. All of the topics treated in chapter 6 would be the way a loving Father would treat his children. In the end, He wants all his children to be with Him.

John Shelby Spong proposes a daring challenge in his book, *The Sins of Scripture*:

> *To step beyond religion is to grow into human maturity. It is to leave behind all of the security boundaries that we have erected against our fears. It is to recognize that the world is so large that differences can be embraced and honored. It is to step beyond tribal boundaries into a new and fuller sense of human identity.[3]*

I find myself more and more removed from traditional church worship and rituals. In examining the seven sacraments of the Catholic Church, I recommend keeping only three of them. The ones that can go away (as they are currently) are Baptism, Confirmation, Holy Orders and Penance. The keepers would be Matrimony, Sacrament of the Sick and the Mass modified from its present form. Here's the rationale for this statement.

Baptism – we are loved unconditionally by God. We do not need to be baptized to be made clean from the stain of sin. We are already in His good graces. This could be changed to a rite of welcoming a new life into the world celebrating the beginning of a person's journey and a new lifetime of possibilities.

Confirmation – we are not soldiers for Christ. Jesus is not looking for martyrs or missionaries but for people to live lives that let their light shine brightly. That is the sermon we all preach. This could be modified to remind us of God's living presence within us as we go forward into adulthood.

Holy Orders – we do not need someone special to mediate our concerns to God. We can communicate with God directly (and always could). The anointed hierarchy and authority structure needs to go away or be revised to reflect a different reality than they do now. A key person in a believing community might just be one who schedules or convenes and plans community events instead of the anointed teacher or tribal leader. Members of a congregation could share spiritual insights for a teaching.

Penance – we are already forgiven by an all-loving God. Just remember the Prodigal Son parable. The father was not at all interested in an accounting from his son of what all he had done. There is nothing we can do to keep God's love from us. Add on to this the concept that there is no place called 'hell or purgatory."

As mentioned, the keepers are as follows:

The Eucharist or Mass – community worship needs to be revisited and reformed if it is to have meaning for future generations and reflect the new spirituality. It clearly needs to reflect the joy and peace of the "good news" that we are in love with a God of unconditional love and become a celebration of who we are.

Matrimony or Marriage – this is an important time in people's lives to be celebrated with a spiritual focus. It is all about love – same sex or heterosexual couples.

Sacrament of the Sick – this is also a key event in everyone's life – transition from our earthly existence to our spiritual home. What a wonderful opportunity to focus on the meaning of a lifetime and its conclusion and the role that person played in the lives of others.

The core issue: What we need to realize and think long and hard about is this: Following a set of rules set out by someone else is not internalizing the Divine invitation to find out what it means to love. Rules are *external motivation* for doing things. We are trying to conform our life to a set of guidelines supposedly set forth by god. The motivation is coming from outside of us – follow the rules and that is all you have to do. An example might be to following the Ten Commandments. Instead of following the rules, we are invited to *internalize* the question of what does it mean to love. This motivation comes from within. It means thinking for ourselves about what it means to love. Following the rules won't buy salvation: living life out or love will.

Where I find myself today: I am more interested in re-writing existing church prayers than I am in reciting them. Yet in the hospital work I am called to do, I realize that those whose lives I touch need a lot of the traditional prayers and language. I can accommodate their needs knowing that in so doing, it is a way of loving them and dealing with what they understand.

Meanwhile, the search for deeper meaning continues. I am enjoying the journey and the questions along the way. What a blessing to have a life partner who understands much of this and puts up with my musings and exploring. We are both avid readers and spiritual seekers. We journey together along life's path. Such a joy! I hope you also have someone who shares your spiritual journey.

I feel that the most important focus I can have in my life right now is to learn as much about the evolving spirituality and the good news. In helping others along that path, we can attain unity with our Creator together, echoing the phrase that "no one enters heaven alone." So we proclaim joy and love by the way we live. I consider this lifetime a success. The awareness I have gained will save several unnecessary lifetimes, I hope. Barbara and I have a wealth of life experiences to learn from (as do all of us) to reflect on what it all means looking back and seeing the spiritual path we walked and how the past got us here.

If you have made it through this chapter, you might find yourself at a decision point on whether to continue with a faith congregation or go it alone. If you decide to stay with a faith community, then be the Jesus of your group and challenge the established ways of doing things that don't make sense. There are viable faith communities that are living the tenets of the Gospel and where the Holy Spirit's work is visible. If you are in one of those and are growing from that association, that is a valid path for you and I commend you for finding a faith community whose light of love shines brightly.

Next is the topic of prayer – the language we use for spiritual communication with this God of unconditional love.

[1] Conversations with God for Teens, by Neale Donald Walsch, (c. 2002), p. 132
[2] God Lives, by James Kavanaugh, (c. 1993), P. 78
[3] Jimmy Carter's letter to the Southern Baptist Convention severing ties with that organization (20)
[4] The Sins of Scripture, by John Shelby Spong, (c. 2005), p. 289

Prayer

*Feeling is the language
that the mind of God recognizes*
- Gregg Braden

No other topic has such a diversity of opinion in faith communities as does "Prayer." It is a complex subject because it involves a lot of "questions such as," "to Whom are we praying?" "Is there a proper way to pray?" "Does God intervene in human affairs?" "Does God even hear my prayer?" "Why are prayers not always answered?"

Traditionally, prayers are prayed to a god we feel can fix a particular problem or respond to a request. The god we pray to we assume can and will intervene into human affairs and bring about the changes we ask for. With the death of this theistic god, the definition of prayer begs to be redefined.

To whom are we praying? Is it someone outside of ourselves or is it the presence of God within us? A person whose god is one of judging, condemnation, vengeance and punishment will pray differently than a person whose God is forgiving, non-judgmental and all loving. Prayer is a very personal communication between us and our Creator or Jesus as the case may be. How a person prays reveals a lot about the God they believe in.

The Ladder of prayer[1]: The quality of prayer has been compared to a ladder. The lowest rung on the ladder of prayer is all about asking for something we don't have or need - perhaps an outcome such as a person being cured of a terrible disease. This level of prayer almost prescribes outcomes or the effect we want to see as the result of our prayer. Prayers of this kind are always for some kind of resolution, something to be fixed. But as we climb the ladder of prayer, the way we do prayer looks quite different at the top than when on the first rung. Now let's take a closer look at the beginning.

Praying out of "lack": This took me some time to understand, but I think it is critical to grasp what this means. A vast majority of our prayers are prayed out of "lack." The clue here is when we pray "for" something or an outcome. We pray for something we don't have yet and so we put that out to the universe (here you can substitute God for the universe). Using the "Law of Attraction" methodology, we visualize and vocalize that for example, we don't have a job. So we lack something and the universe responds in kind by verifying that lack; it mirrors what we give it. We still won't have a job when that's what we visualize. Visualization is the first step. So as long as we visualize lack, that's what we'll have. Many petitions in worship services are prayed from a sense of lack. We don't go to the next steps of visualizing fulfillment and giving thanks. We can pray for world peace, but without visualizing a world at peace and thanking God that it is so in advance, we fall short of effective prayer. Praying out of lack is like saying, "I need this – please help." *A Course in Miracles* describes this as the bottom rung of "the ladder of prayer." It is the lowest form of prayer and the least effective.

When you think about it, many of the psalms and most of our prayers are prayed from a sense of lack.

> *How much longer will you forget me? How much longer will you hide your face from me? How much longer must I endure grief in my soul, and sorrow in my heart by day and by night...Look and answer me, Yahweh my God!"* (Ps. 13).

Praying from a sense of lack comes from thinking that god will come in and set all things right; that he has the power to do so leaves us wondering why god doesn't come in and fix things. The theistic god is thought to intervene in human affairs. First here are some examples of that process.

The Book of Revelation seems to personify and feed heavily on this idea. In the end, god will come and intervene with judgment finally bringing justice to an ailing world. It is a nice thought, but it isn't going to happen. Jesus' second coming will not be so unlike his first. That is why the god of conditional love concept is so out of step with what God is really like. God cannot be what He/She is not, e.g. be judgmental, vindictive and punishing.

It has always seemed silly to me to embrace that god cares who wins a particular athletic contest and praying for a team to win seemed like a non-prayer. Often in an interview, the player of a winning team that made a crucial play to win the game gives credit to a god guiding the football through the uprights from 63 yards out. Is it not more likely that his talents and long hours of practice made that possible? The same goes with believers on both sides of a war praying for victory. Would not praying for peace have been a more appropriate prayer?

So much of our prayer seem to revolve around the notion that god is going to step in and correct a bad situation. When shooting deaths occur in cities, prayer walks are often organized. Prayer walks are fine and maybe they are praying for the victim's family. I don't know, but it seems like getting together to pray makes the participants feel better. Sometimes prayer is for the "pray-ers." I don't know how much good it does to correct the underlying causes.

Praying that a hurricane headed for your town be diverted strikes an interesting note. Are the pray-ers praying that the hurricane will visit its destruction on another inhabited area and not in their own back yard? This notion also seems like a disingenuous kind of prayer to me. Would it be better to pray that the destructive force of the storm subside?

Praying for specific outcomes smacks of telling god how to answer our petitions – a bit presumptuous it seems. Do we really know what the best outcome should be? There is always more going on for a soul than we observe in this life.

> *Prayer is perhaps one of the most ancient and mysterious of human experiences. It's also the most personal.*
> -Gregg Braden

For me, prayer evolved. Growing up in Catholic schools, a lot of my prayer was petitioning god for certain outcomes; be it passing a test, asking for forgiveness in the confessional or that I get that bicycle I wanted. In many ways, god was analogous to Santa Claus. He knew everything I did and that someday, I would have to come to terms with what I did or didn't do. So there were sins of "commission" and sins of "omission." I can't say that I was afraid of god, but neither was he friendly. This perspective probably was with me through my high school years.

Evolving notion of prayer: Going up the ladder, the next rung is prayer placing the outcome in the hands of God. From my experiences in working with the sick and dying at the hospital, I am often asked to pray with the family of the deceased or pray with patients. The hospital experience puts one's concept of prayer to the test. These situations raise questions regarding prayer. What do I pray for? What should I not pray for? What does the patient need to hear? What does the family of the deceased need to hear? These questions have served to examine how I attend to families and patients.

In the case of a sudden death in the emergency department, it is a challenge to come up with words that will comfort someone who is deeply grieving over the loss. I don't attempt to explain why this happened. The truth is none of us knows why. In the case of a heart attack, if I pray for complete recovery and the patient dies, that prayer seems to be unanswered or perceived as ineffective. The truth is that the patient's soul's agenda and Divine plan for that person is what will determine the outcome. So I can pray that the patient be granted the strength and inner peace to get through this. I can also pray that the patient's future be placed in God's hands, who only wants what is best for him/her. I can pray for those attending to the patient to be granted the grace to accept the outcome and be at peace with it. Instead of trying to make sense out of what is happening, we can pray that the matter be placed in the hands of a higher power. So our prayer is to simply recognize what "is" and place that in the hands of God knowing that such will be the best outcome.

What is clear to everyone is that now begins a new chapter in their lives. That is again a matter of the soul's agenda working in concert with God. It is all happening for a reason beyond what we can understand. I simply acknowledge the fact that none of us understand the events of this day and acknowledge the feelings people have because of what happened.

All feelings are ok – they are part of the grieving process. Usually after a period of time, those left behind come to the realization that "it is what it is" and that they need to focus on what needs to be done to go on and that God is attending to the needs of the deceased. At that time, they are more open to prayer then when they first came in.

Above all, I have come to recognize every person as a precious child of God. Each is part of the magnificent Sonship of our Creator and worthy of special treatment. I pray that I can be the face of compassion to the lives I touch and see every encounter as a holy experience. So once again, a spirituality brought to life's experiences has helped my concept of prayer evolve further.

Gratitude: Further up the ladder of prayer is being grateful. I cannot over-emphasize how important this is.

Gratitude should be the foundation of any valid spirituality. How much of our prayer is gratitude and thankfulness for many things? I believe that a quality prayer is one that includes gratitude to our Creator. What am I grateful for? About everything – another day to get it right, another day with my bride and our life together, that we can put food on the table, for those who had a hand in getting it there, for friends and neighbors, for the insights we have asked for and received. There are a ton of things to be grateful for. To get in the "gratitude" habit, some recommend at the end of the day to keep a log of all the things a person is grateful for that day.

Being grateful for the challenges that life presents, its problems, trials and tribulations is a leap that is hard to make. Those are the growing opportunities, not problems and they come to us for a reason. It may be a long shot to understand why losing a spouse or being severely injured in a traffic accident is an opportunity for growth, but there is a reason why things like that happen. Just thank God for this opportunity and be open to what you can learn from it. Maybe it can be seen more clearly in hindsight. Having cancer twice now, has been a learning occasion for others and me. Another example may be a painful divorce or the death of a spouse was the means to a more meaningful and loving relationship with another. It is hard to see where the experience of a problem is leading when going through it, but looking back, it seems to have the fingerprints of the Holy Spirit all over it. So seeing all of life, the very gift of life as something to be grateful for is a sign of progress on the ladder of prayer.

Neale Donald Walsch in his book, *Conversations with God* series, echoes these sentiments a little more forcefully in the following excerpt:

> *The correct prayer is therefore never a prayer of supplication, but a prayer of gratitude.*
>
> *When you thank God in advance for that which you choose to experience in your reality, you, in effect, acknowledge that it is there...in effect. Thankfulness is thus the most powerful statement to God, an affirmation that even before you ask, I have answered. Therefore never supplicate. Appreciate.*[2]

Praying from fulfillment: At the top of the ladder of prayer is praying out of our emotions or feelings. We can gain some insight into praying from the "Law of Attraction" methodology using visualization. This is where we pray from the mind and the heart together in unison. People visualize themselves getting that job they want or meeting the right person as a life partner, etc. They see themselves where the desire is fulfilled and experience the feelings associated with that fulfilled realization. In other words, they see it as already done and accomplished even though when they visualize this, none of it has been fulfilled. It is a way of putting it out to the universe so that the universe will respond in kind. This is praying out of a sense of fulfillment, seeing it realized in the future and thanking God in advance.

Gregg Braden, a popular spiritual author shared a real life experience of how this works in his book, *Secrets of the Lost Art of Prayer.*[3] A Native American friend invited him to go and "pray rain." There had been a serious drought in his area. Gregg jumped at the opportunity and together they hiked to a sacred prayer site up in the hills. When they arrived at the prayer circle, his friend took off his shoes and stepped into a stone circle laid out on the ground. He thanked all his ancestors that had gone before him (thanking those who made his life possible); he offered thanks to the four winds and the benefits they brought (a way of recognizing the Earth we are connect to). Then he assumed a prayerful silence using no spoken words. After a few minutes, he stepped out of the circle and asked Gregg if he wanted to get something to eat. Gregg was puzzled about the silent part of the prayer ritual.

His friend explained that during that time, he envisioned what it is like when it rains only he talked about it in terms of emotions and the five sensual experiences. He envisioned what rain smells like and the joy of seeing the rain. He saw himself walking through tall fields of corn because there was enough water and what the corn tasted like on his table. He heard the sound of the rain as it fell to the ground and on the sidewalls of his hut and what it's like to stand out in the rain. He felt the moist earth between his toes. It was the feelings that went along with the visualizations that were the prayer. No words were needed or spoken. This is another example of praying from fulfillment. The prayer was effective – rains came a couple days later that flooded the streets. Gregg said that this was the art of praying that was part of the ancient wisdom of our ancestors, which was lost over time but preserved in the traditions of this native culture. The Native American didn't say, "Come with me to pray for rain" instead he wanted to "pray rain." He simply left out the "for" which indicated lack.

Another example of fulfillment is always the answer the Holy Spirit delivers. It is always a win/win for all parties concerned. Barbara and I wanted a Holy Spirit resolution in a real-estate matter. In 2006, we decided to sell the house we had lived in for 30 years. Our prayer was that all parties concerned would come out winners. What does that mean? It means that we would get a price that we wanted; that the buyer would get the parcel of land that he/she wanted for that price; that the person who would be selling the home we would be moving into would be able to sell for a price that we both liked and that the timing would work out for them as well as us; that the seller of the home that they were going to buy would get what they wanted. At that time we also included the city that wanted a portion of our land to straighten the roadway. That seemed like a lot of pieces and demands to place at the feet of the Holy Spirit asking for a miracle, but when you pray that way, be prepared.

We got the price we were asking, the buyer got his parcel and already had a plan to build condos on it, the seller of the home we decided on accepted our offer and they had enough resources to build a new condo. We had three weeks between the closing and moving into our next home – three weeks to start moving stuff between the two places. By the way, the City negotiated with the new owner and got the land they sought. All of this happened before the market took the downward slide in 2008.

This will also hold true when praying for our enemies. We must include them in the Holy Spirit's solution that they be included in a positive outcome (let the Holy Spirit decide what that might be).

Gregg Braden wrote a book, *Secrets of the Lost Mode of Prayer*. He has done extensive research on ancient wisdom. He found that over the centuries, scriptural documents have been edited and as a result, some of the original meaning was lost. In the following example, Jesus instructed us in John 16:23-24 to, "ask and you shall receive." But the versions of scripture that we have today have left out an important line or two that instructs us on "how" to ask. So, here is what we have today from the King James Version:

> *Whatsoever ye ask the Father in my name, He will give it to you. Hitherto have ye asked nothing in my name: Ask and ye shall receive, that your joy may be full.*

By re-translating from the original manuscripts, it is clear what was edited out through the centuries and the liberties taken in translation. Here is the original text:

> *All things that you ask straightly, directly...from inside my name, you will be given. So far you have not done this. Ask without hidden motive and be surrounded by your answer. Be enveloped by what you desire, that your gladness may be full.*[4]

That sounds to me like instructions to pray in fulfillment. So when someone asks, "Teach me how to pray?" it is not a simple question.

Unanswered Prayers: Most all of us have had an experience where we felt a sincerely expressed prayer went unanswered. What we perceive as unanswered prayers may not be the case. Perhaps we were praying out of "lack." Maybe they are answered but not in the way we were expecting. Sometimes it is because we have asked for the impossible - something God will not or cannot grant. If the action we seek involves punishing another or that someone gets their just rewards or getting your team to win, etc., then we have to realize that God doesn't punish or have a favorite team. God cannot do what God is not. God is love and all God's actions are out of love, not fear or any other motive. Judgment and punishment are not what an all-loving God is about. God would never do or grant anything that would engender fear or retribution.

A Course in Miracles suggests that all prayer is answered. We have received the answer but possibly haven't heard or seen it. When we ask the Holy Spirit for anything, we will get a response. But we can also be certain that a God given response won't be one that increases fear.

Meditation: When meditation is mentioned, people tend to cringe. It doesn't sound like something that fits their lifestyle. Meditation, though, has a multitude of forms. There are walking meditations where the walker simply marvels at all that nature produces. It has elements of gratitude appreciating beauty. Meditation most commonly is a quieting of the thoughts of the mind – to clear the mind of the clutter of the many thoughts that go through our heads all day long so that another voice can be heard. Insights come when the mind is not cluttered. Meditation does not need to take a lot of time to do. In the morning five or ten minutes will do. It can be a purposeful thinking of a theme of the morning reading or a clearing of thoughts and experiencing a feeling of gratitude for whatever comes to mind. I am not an expert on meditation by any means, but the Morning Prayer routine is my best space to take some quiet time to reflect on a reading.

Praying miracles: Notice I didn't say, "pray for miracles." The most effective miracle is changing our perceptions or adopting new beliefs that are more inclusive. That is what the miracle means in the title *A Course in Miracles*. It is all about changing the way we see ourselves, and the world we live in. But miracles also occur in broad daylight when you approach your day "expecting" a miracle.

A case in point is this example. In our morning reading, it was suggested that we expect a miracle that day. So we said, "OK, we'll do that and look for one." As it happened, the occasion was a PT Scan during my treatments for cancer. These usually take 2-3 hours with the preparation and the scan. Barbara was sitting out in the waiting area for that time when she heard someone say, "Barb?" It turned out to be a distant cousin that she had not seen for 40 years. They sat and talked for an hour.

Just out of the blue it happened. But it didn't stop there. The next day she connected with a couple at the hospital that was willing to help with our used book sale we do once a month. They love books, are avid readers and our crew needs some younger blood. The following day, she found another person interested in joining our "No One Dies Alone" team. The key is to pray and expect miracles and thank God in advance.

For Barbara and me, the greatest miracles have occurred in the area of spirituality and the evolving nature of the Holy Spirit's guidance. We have traveled so far spiritually from where we were growing up. It is important to ask for wisdom to find your path to your truth - those things that resonate in your heart; visualize having that with feeling and thank God in advance.

Praying others: It is proper to visualize others in prayer. The Bible admonishes that we even include our enemies. One thought that has helped me with this is that there are no "loser" souls, only good souls who have lost their way. We are all here trying to find our way home. We know that earth is a temporary residence for all of us and that we need all the help we can get. *A Course in Miracles* puts it this way: *"No one is crucified alone and no one enters heaven alone."* We are here to help each other and including others in prayer is another way to help. We gain heaven by helping others find their way and in the same way, when we put someone else down, we diminish ourselves. We often don't know what loads others may be carrying in life. So pray for others – visualize them in a better place and thank God in advance. Much can be said about praying and how to pray but in the end, the learning is in practicing the art of prayer – doing it.

My journey with the ladder of prayer: When I entered the seminary after high school, my first four years did little to change my belief except that god became more of a curiosity for me knowing that I was training to be the "intermediary" for a Christian community someday. It was still a theistic notion that I maintained at its core. The next four years at a theological seminary brought some further challenges to my concept of god, in the sense that I was definitely examining what the role of the priest, who was god's representative and intermediary for the believing community, was all about.

It wasn't until I was ordained and officially a member of the Roman Catholic hierarchy that I really had to look at what I was doing and saying as my faith was on display for all to see. I can honestly say that my six years in the active ministry was a constant evolution of what I believed and professed. I had to find meaning in the confessions I heard, the Masses I said and the other sacraments at which I officiated. I had to find meaning or I couldn't continue to mechanically perform those rituals. So it still had meaning for me to say, "Lord have mercy" and to acknowledge that I had my faults, call them sins of commission or whatever and to petition God for forgiveness for myself and the worshipping community. But the longer I served in this capacity, the more aware I became that fostering guilt was part of those rituals. I believed the theistic god of conditional love lived in those sacraments. At this point, I was having problems with the concept of "mortal sin" which was a very serious sin. If one died before getting to confession, this would mean serious consequences in the afterlife – at one point - hell for all eternity. Not a pleasant thought, but it seemed a cruel god who would do that. I also believed in multiple lifetimes and that helped with several theological questions I had. So my beliefs were evolving and my satisfaction with the duties of the active ministry was diminishing as well. I became more impatient with the politics of the Catholic Church and the fact that celibacy was a strong tenet of the priesthood. By this time I had found much meaning in ministering directly to people and felt the Spirit at work in those relationships, but in the end, my dissatisfaction with the church in general won out.

I left the active ministry in 1975. For a while after that I attended Sunday masses and left disappointed in their content and eventually quit going all together. So now I was without an association with a faith community and with a lot of questions that had to do with prayer.

My ideas about prayer have continued to evolve since that time. Through reading, observation and experience, prayer has become more meaningful, effective and focused.

Praying wisdom: So in closing, I offer the following prayer:

May the Father of all who loves you no matter what - guide you to realize the goals that you have set for this lifetime so that when you breathe your last, you will feel at peace in that it was not a lifetime wasted but one where miracles happened. May the peace that the world cannot give be yours – may your joy be complete to shine away any darkness that you may see clearly the path you need to follow. Know that God's will is your will, for God wants only what is best for you. I visualize your joy and happiness in your new-found insights. Rest in that promise and I thank God in advance. Amen.

Prayer is an integral part of living well. Knowing how to die well means living life well with few regrets. We all want to look back on a life well lived, so this is addressed next.

---

[1] Full text is found in A Song of Prayer – a supplement of A Course in Miracles, (c. 1977)
[2] Conversations With God, by Neale Donald Walsch, (c. 1995), p. 11
[3] Secrets of the Lost Mode of Prayer, by Gregg Braden, (c. 2006), p. 12
[4] Secrets of the Lost Mode of Prayer, by Gregg Braden, (c. 2006), p. 132

9

Living Well - Dying Well

Real love is full of living and dying:
It takes the best that a person is because
it takes all that a person is.
— Eugene Kennedy, MM

Nothing gets our attention more than death. It might be hearing of someone we know who has died. It might be receiving a terminal medical diagnosis. It starts to become personal when someone close to us – perhaps a family member – dies suddenly. It is possible that someone you know who is in good health has only two days to live before a fatal traffic accident. It seems that we are never quite prepared for the news of death. Yet death is the punctuation point, the period that comes at the end of a lifetime. It is so final, so irreversible.

We tend to live life unmindful of the reality of death. None of us knows when that moment will come for us but, of course, it definitely will. It doesn't have to be something dreaded or fearful but nevertheless strikes fear in most of us. Would it be beneficial to live life with the end in mind? We can learn a lot from hospice patients who know that they have only so much time left and what they do with it. People with a fatal diagnosis are in an envious position in one sense. They have some time to tie up some loose ends that life has given them. Every day becomes precious – none is wasted. It is a time to look back on life and try to understand what it all means. Having time to say goodbye can be seen as a blessing - to forgive and be at peace when their final moment comes. So to die well, one must live life well.

Living life well means waking up grateful for the gift of another day. It means realizing that love is the only thing that counts for anything in life. We may be very successful in our chosen vocation in life, but if what we do is not done out of a loving motive, we will have wasted precious time. Life on earth can offer a myriad of distractions. A lot of it is just taking care of business such as paying the bills, making appointments or fixing the car. It is just doing what needs to be done.

But in the midst of all that, where the rubber meets the road in life is in our relationships with people. How we manage those relationships is where the stuff of salvation is found. The spiritual work of our life is located here. In end-of-life situations, regrets that people experience have to do with relationships, often, family relationships. One of the goals of hospice is to suggest to the dying that where regrets exist, some healing can still take place in the time left. If not healed in this lifetime, the next lifetime will provide another opportunity. So what is involved in healing relationships?

Forgiveness: This is a tough word for some to swallow. We should be practicing this in our daily lives. Religious and spiritual writers remind us that forgiveness is important. Forgiveness is the power of healing. It is letting go of blame. It is letting go of anger. It is not letting disagreements stew inside you, festering and eating away at your peace of mind. It is letting go of expectations of another, expecting them to change. It is suspending judgment. It is realizing that whatever it was doesn't really matter. It is realizing that what we saw in the other we also see in ourselves. We all have failings or faults. If we can see and forgive our failings and faults, it is easier to apply the same to others. It echoes the greatest commandment, "love your neighbor as you love yourself."

This is especially difficult when someone offends or violates your trust again and again. Forgiveness does not have to be mutual. All we can do is our part and forgive another – to regain our peace of mind by not expecting them to be any different and dealing with our own feelings and resentments. It has everything to do with our expectations of another. Zukav further elaborates:

> *When you feel you have been betrayed by someone, it is because you have expectations about that person that he or she did not fulfill. Forgiving means letting go of those expectations. If you say to yourself that you have forgiven someone, but you haven't let go of your expectations, your forgiveness is not really forgiveness.*[1]

A Couse in Miracles states that our salvation is found in forgiving others and ourselves. There is no shortage of the failings we see in others. So we have multiple opportunities to practice forgiveness. Why wait until the end-of-life to exercise forgiveness? Regardless of what we think of others, I believe that most people think that they are doing the right thing themselves even when we see that what they are doing is wrong or destructive. It doesn't mean that we approve of their actions, but it helps to suspend judgment that they are doing it out of "evil," hateful intentions.

Forgiveness can be extended to those who are no longer with us, who are dead and gone. Grievances we had with a deceased parent can be forgiven in real time by us. All we can do in any forgiveness situation is to do our part. We can only offer our forgiveness. What if the other person doesn't forgive us? What the other person does is not our responsibility. We can change our minds and can't change the minds of others. They have their forgiveness responsibilities.

In looking at our lives, what unresolved relationship issues are there? These are the flags that beg forgiveness. Better to address them now than when time runs out. My goal is to get to the end of life with few if any regrets, in other words, to live life well.

How we look at life's problems and how we feel and deal with them is the issue. If I could go back in time and write a letter to my younger self, say at age 14, I would include the insights I wrote to my godchild upon nearing his adulthood at that same age:

> *Dearest Quinn,*
>
> *At your baptism and as your godfather, I started a book that I hope you will keep with you as you live out the years ahead. It begins with family members and friends writing their thoughts as you were fresh to this world and recently baptized. Then in the*

years following, I added entries in the hopes that lessons I have learned in life, I could pass on to you for your consideration.

As of this writing, I am 74, and have had many life experiences. Life will have some experiences in store for you as it has for all of us. **They are nothing to be afraid of***, but knowing how to look at them is very important. It could be your first car accident, an unexpected health issue, the loss of a family member or friend, losing a job, relationship problems, etc. They will come in many costumes, but when they occur, be sure to see them as an opportunity rather than a problem to be solved. It may be a problem to deal with but it is also a learning opportunity; to gain some insights that make you stronger and you will come out a stronger person.*

I have now had two bouts with cancer, for example, and I learned a lot from this last one and luckily, it was one that I recovered from. One of the things I learned is that I need to do more work on my diet, exercise and the foods and things I eat and drink. I also learned to be grateful for experiences that I can survive. I also learned how important support from family and friends is during a serious illness or disability.

Life lessons are what these are called and we each have our own lessons to grow from. We came here to Earth for this purpose; that is what our lives are about along with what we can do to make this world a better place.

So when something interrupts your ordinary life routines, pay attention and ask yourself, "How can I look at this event? Can I keep a positive attitude and what can I learn from this?" This information is also helpful when your family or friends are going through their life lessons. You can offer them support and stand by them.

Anyway, as you approach adulthood in a few short years, I offer these thoughts hopefully to save you some grief when these events happen to you or someone else. Don't be afraid of life. It is an adventure! Enjoy all that life offers.

My prayer is that you will be able to look back on your life and be able to say, "I have learned a lot from life and have few regrets. Life is worth living." With love,
Poppa

The Death Experience: Some are afraid of dying and others are more afraid of the suffering that leads to dying. The scary part of dying is that all that we are about here in this lifetime is about to be left behind. We know what it is to be alive, but not at all sure about what happens after. What this means is that after death, the role of father/mother, friendships, possessions and wealth, a professional role, religious affiliation, are left behind. The familiar is left behind. We fear death and what happens after it; judgment will be rendered and justice meted out. This is the idea of death that many learned growing up.

On the other hand, a person who had died is free of any physical handicap, disease, debts owed, depression, mental illness and any legal messes that they experienced in this lifetime. After death, the soul returns to its natural spiritual state. I find it comforting to reflect that when a person with terminal cancer dies, that soul is totally free of any pain, physical disability and suffering. These are all related to the body. None of these exist in the life of the spirit. The soul is free of limitations and fully conscious. Death can be a liberating experience. What is ahead seems unknown and fearful but there are many accounts of incidents where a person near death sees someone familiar in the room that others don't see. They may be talking to them and comforting them.

Those who have had near-death experiences (who have died and been revived) share their experiences of what it was like to die. Almost all relate a pleasant and even joyful experience out of the body. They felt loved and safe. They also had conversations from the spirit side that told them that it was not their time yet. They had to return. They felt free of any suffering and felt reluctant to return to the body, but knew that they must - that there was more work here for them to do. They relate that they are no longer afraid to die and the scariness of dying is no longer of concern to them. That should be somewhat reassuring to know that there is help after we leave this planet. In a sense, we are never alone.

Planning for a Death Experience

Before: Since death is an event scheduled for all of us, advance planning is advisable. After all, we plan for all other major life events. Why not plan for our death? Some preparations ahead of time can be beneficial to family members. Signing up for life insurance for the surviving spouse is one example. Specifying in writing who gets what after you are gone can save some family strife. Making advanced funeral arrangements and even prepay whenever possible takes some of the burden off family members. Planning your funeral service with songs, readings, presider of the service, etc. can also make things easier for family left behind.

You can even specify what you want and don't want at end of life. An advanced directive is a document, a medical directive outlining procedures you want or don't want when you can't speak for yourself. A medical Power of Attorney is a legal document designating someone who can make medical decisions on your behalf when you can't. A financial Power of Attorney is another document to have in place. These make decision making easier for family and also medical staff attending to you. You do them a favor by having these in place. There have been some unhappy and argumentative situations causing family strife that have happened when these were not done.

Things to consider here are whether or not you want to be resuscitated if your heart stops; do you want CPR performed or to be intubated (breathing tube and resuscitator). Do you want Hospice involved at end of life? What pain management do you want (palliative care)? Having done much of this, I feel much better about what my family will experience when my time comes.

Attending the dying: As mentioned before, I am part of a team that attends the dying who have no family or friends locally who can be with them in their final hours. We formed our local "No One Dies Alone" program in 2009. Team members attend the dying during their estimated last 48 hours of life. Our goal is to help them make a good transition from this life to the spirit side. We have learned a lot about death and dying in doing this. We no longer fear death but have learned to respect the dying process. It is a special time in the life of that person and a privilege to be there and share in that moment. Most of the time the patient is comatose and is not able to interact consciously with us, but we feel we can communicate with them through prayer and thought. Our message is reassuring. In short, God loves you regardless of what you did in this life. Do not be afraid. It is ok to go when you are ready. You are a precious child of God and you will be welcomed home after you die. This is your temporary home here. The body gradually declines and death usually comes peacefully for most. It is like going to sleep and waking up on the other side greeted by someone you know or have known.

After: Birth and death are similar. They are both transitions. Souls on the spirit side hand a person off to earthly parents at birth. We say good-bye on the earthly side when the soul transitions to the spirit realm. There are souls on the spirit side that will assist us to readjust to the life in spirit form, just as it took some time for our parents and families to get us used to being human as we matured. After death, some relate that the soul of the deceased visits loved ones to say good-bye. Loved ones may not realize this is happening on a conscious level, but do on a soul level. I believe there is some truth that we attend our own funerals in spirit form to comfort loved ones. We become less and less concerned about the affairs of our earthly existence and more focused on doing the work between lifetimes. Just to recap, that involves a review of the recently completed life lived to see what planning we want to incorporate into the design of the next lifetime. We will be reunited with loved ones that have preceded us in death.

In the end, living well is having a reverence for life in all its aspects; seeing that all forms of life exist for a reason and purpose. It means treating all forms of life with respect – respect for the Earth itself. It means valuing relationships with all of mankind regardless of race, country, language or culture. It means seeing evidence of the Divine in all of creation, especially in the beauty of the human species. If we can live well, dying will be embraced with acceptance and inner peace.

---

[1] The Seat of the Soul, by Gary Zukav, (c. 1989), p. 185

Charting Your Own Course

*Few ask for the grace to give up
what has been for what could be.*
- A Course of Love, T VI,6:6,1

    This chapter is a guide for those who seek a vibrant spirituality that is not connected with a faith community or church.

    When I decided to leave the active ministry, I wondered if God would be ok with my decision to get out of full-time dedication to His ministry. But I knew I had to leave behind what had been – the active ministry – for something yet undetermined. I soon learned that spiritual guidance had not left me. Looking back, I was shown opportunities in looking for work and meeting people who would help me along the way.

    I attended Sunday Masses for a while right after I left. The issues that surrounded my decision to leave were still there and I would leave a bit angry. But after a while, I quit going all together. Looking at things from the outside only revealed the truth that my decision was the right one for me.

    Now I was looking for what "could be." At age 33, not knowing what was ahead was also a bit unsettling, but not enough to want to go back to the active ministry. Now, some 40 plus years later, I am convinced that the Holy Spirit was in the picture all along and that the path I've walked has all been as it should be to bring me to where I am today. It all feels right.

The most significant event for me was finding, falling in love and marrying Barbara. She also had issues with the Catholic Church at the time we met. We have shared our search for a meaningful spirituality together for years now. We are in love with the God of unconditional love. Life and gratitude is our spiritual orientation. We are the happiest we have ever been and are ready to leave the planet whenever that time comes. To share a life journey later in life is a precious gift that we are grateful for daily.

I had made the choice to place my future in the hands of the God I had found and implicitly trusted that all would be for the best. I believe that is the first step – unconditional trust. Along with that, I have confidence in myself to figure things out, to make good decisions and choices in life. There is a peace that comes with being on the outside of an organization with a Divine assurance that things are ok. I discovered that I no longer needed a "mediator", a priest, imam, minister or shaman to interpret for me or to intercede on my behalf. I can discern what a loving choice or action is and organize my life around those decisions. I also learned that there is an unlimited source of help available from our spirit guides and teachers if I but asked them. So the bottom line is that the life that has been given us is the important activity we can engage in during this incarnation. It is not **what** we do in life that counts – as is **how** we do it. Do we project love or judgment? This is the opportunity to learn the life lessons we have come here for. I invite you to make the most of the time you have.

The first thing is being ok with who we are. Being a person of integrity is the goal in any lifetime. If we are tortured with guilt and fear, integrity is in jeopardy and that is what we will project out to others instead of a response based in love.

Miguel Ruiz has suggested that there are five agreements that we should make with ourselves that will go a long way in guiding us through life. They are psychological goals that need to be practiced daily and have spiritual implications. Being our authentic selves is life's challenge.[1]

First agreement is be impeccable with your word. Do what you say you will do and what you will not do. Never put yourself down for the things you do or say. We all make mistakes and we can always choose again and do things differently.

Second agreement is don't take anything personally. We all see the world and life events through our own colored glasses. The way someone else sees or reacts to us has everything to do with what is going on for them. If you didn't intentionally set out to hurt them, then why should you internalize their anger and feel bad? It is like depositing a poison into your system when there is no need to. Thoughts can fester and stew in one's mind and the goal is to keep that at a minimum. Excessive emotional stress can kill. Be in control of your thoughts: you may not have any control over what thoughts come into your mind, but you can control how long they stay there. Having a good opinion of one's self quickly sees through this problem.

The third agreement is don't make assumptions. We all make assumptions that everyone sees life the way we do. Each of us filters life's experiences through different lenses. If we don't always understand something, it is better to ask and be clear.

The fourth agreement is always do your best in any circumstance in your life. It doesn't matter if you are sick or tired, if you always do your best; there is no way you can judge yourself. And if you don't judge yourself, there is no way you are going to suffer from guilt, blame or self-punishment. The goal is to live without regrets.

The fifth agreement is the agreement that I live my life by - to question everything you are asked to believe and discover what is true for you. In other words, have the courage to question and modify your beliefs as you go through life. This is where the work of salvation occurs – living a life of integrity with few if any regrets.[2]

The goal of the new spirituality is to eliminate barriers to love. The God of unconditional love offers freedom from fear and guilt and with these two main barriers gone, we can discover the joy and peace that comes from knowing the **God Who IS** and not the one that man thought god was.

Guides and Teachers: There is a wealth of help and resources available to us all as we search to find our truth. There are spirit guides and teachers that we can call upon and receive guidance about a problem we face or a decision we must make. To access this resource, we need to ask for it and then listen for answers.

Cheryl Richardson, a life coach, wrote a book *The Unmistakable Touch of Grace* that I highly recommend. She advises her clients to ask for help with the following prayer:

> *I am now open and receptive to the power of grace in my life. I ask to be shown clear examples of how I can face this challenge with courage, wisdom and strength.*[3]

The book is filled with numerous examples of how such a prayer was answered.

Another author, Doreen Virtue offers a similar prayer:

> *Dearest God, I ask You to enter my dreams tonight and clear away the fears that keep me from understanding, trusting, and following Divine guidance. If there is a message You wish to give me, please help me to understand clearly and remember it in the morning. Thank You and Amen*[4]

Answers can come in all sorts of ways. The key is to be keenly aware of everything after you ask. Answers can come in hearing lyrics to a song, seeing a movie, an overheard conversation, an unexpected phone call, thoughts and ideas that come into your mind, a dream, a job offer, a new friend, a new activity, a recommended book, etc. You get the picture – answers come in a myriad of ways. You will have all the direction you need and won't miss the group think of organized religion. Be ok with where you are: without a religious affiliation, you are free to discover spiritual truths that will resonate with you and be your truth. Remember what others think may be helpful only if it resonates with your inner spirit. The same can be said for this book. Take what resonates with you and don't worry about the rest.

Find a context for your spirituality: We interact and relate to other people in our world. In all those relationships our spirituality touches the lives of others. You can look at life as ministering to others and they to us. We are social creatures and need cooperative relationships for good mental health and for a good spirituality. For my wife and me, the hospital community provides that need. It is there that our lives cross with others and it is an opportunity to help others through a spiritual crisis. It is a meaningful and important time to be involved in their lives.

Every relationship provides an opportunity for growing spiritually. It is in connecting with others that we can learn and give. Every relationship should be considered a holy encounter with another child of our Father. Even if you are sick or homebound, there are still people with whom you come in contact. Communications as they are today with the Internet and cell phones, there are still ways to connect with others. There are numerous opportunities for volunteering in your community. Pick one that is of interest to you and get involved and establish relationships. My wife and I put on a used book sale in the hospital lobby once a month. That has been a vehicle to connect with families of patients. We often are a safe and welcomed listening ear for someone who needs to talk. Besides loving books, we thoroughly enjoy those days.

If you know of someone who has cancer or some debilitating disease and is hurting, consider that there is a good possibility that they are feeling somewhat isolated from the community and a phone call means the world to them. It is a way to connect with them and them with you. I can tell you that it's true because when I had lymphatic cancer in 2017, personal contact was highly valued. At the recommendation of my son, a website was developed so I could share with friends and family some of the experiences and lessons I learned from that medical episode. It was another way of connecting spiritually. Websites like Caring Bridge and Posthope are designed for this purpose.

Your support system: When you likely belonged to a faith community or church, you were with people who supported your beliefs. You felt confident and comfortable there. Now, when considering living life without a church community, you still need souls who think along similar lines. You meet people like this if you are looking for them. Surround yourself with those who support you or are on a similar spiritual path, but also include some who will be honest and give you advice when needed. These are people who reflect the divine presence to you. These are the people who bring joy into your life. Joy is a sign of God's presence in any person or group. Ask in prayer to find these souls who more than likely are also looking for mutual support.

When the world around us presents us daily with little joy, this becomes necessary.

Spiritual Food: In today's world, there is a wealth of information in print, audio, DVD, and on the Internet. Barb and I are avid readers. Over the years I have collected portions of texts from various authors that have helped shape my belief system and also challenged me spiritually. This database is the treasure trove of information from which I drew to do this book. Our minds and souls need to be fed quality materials to remain alive and healthy.

If reading is not what you're into, many of the authors sited in this work also have videos on YouTube. There are some websites I would recommend as resources that will keep you up to date on current thinking. These are listed under the recommended reading list. Having worked with the sick and dying, I am naturally interested in end of life issues. I want to know all I can about the dynamics of the soul's experiences, to find my central truth - peace within so when my time comes, I will not be afraid of dying but accept that experience gracefully. One expression I heard is, "the best day of your life is when it ends." That is when we leave all the cares of this world behind. I want to make the most of the time I have on this planet and this lifetime to learn as much as I can and to evolve in my spiritual understanding. I make no secret that I am cramming for the final exam and having access to information is a big part of that process.

There's no excuse for not having a spiritual practice in your life. It means doing something that puts you in touch with the spiritual. If organized religion isn't your thing, then you have the responsibility to develop a spiritual practice – something that centers you and calms the noise of the world. It might be a walk in nature where you find the Divine presence. Transcendental meditation is another way. It doesn't have to be even attending any kind of spiritual based meeting, but it could also mean that – whatever works for you - anything that will keep you in touch with your soul's goal of evolving spiritually. It is your reason for being here. By doing this, you will find that inner peace and joy that we all long for and that the world cannot give. Having spiritual issues to think about also keeps the mind active and healthy. So make sure you feed your spirit. These authors cited in this work, in my opinion, reflect the work of the Holy Spirit seeking to reach those who are ready for a spiritual awakening; they are living it. I invite you to check the books and websites listed in the appendix. The new spirituality is very available to those who choose to seek and find.

Listen to your Heart: The best guide for any of us is to follow our gut feelings or thinking with our hearts instead of our minds. The mind will sometimes sabotage what we should do by overthinking it. In the end, it is what we are comfortable with and feel we are doing the best thing. If you have a life decision facing you, ask your guides for spiritual guidance and then listen intently. If what you receive is in line with your gut feeling, you will likely have your answer. Life does not have to be complicated. Don't try to go it alone. Ask for guidance, insights and wisdom. Take comfort that even if you make a decision that you regret, there is always another chance to get it right. If you find that what you decided isn't working for you, then choose again – make another choice and try not to stay in a destructive situation. Your Father honors all choices and knows that we always have another chance to get it right.

---

[1] The Four Agreements, by Miguel Ruiz, (c. 1997), Points are summarized from this book
[2] The Fifth Agreement, by Miguel Ruiz, (c. 2010), Point is summarized from this book
[3] The Unmistakable Touch of Grace, by Cheryl Richardson, (c. 2005), p. 72
[4] Divine Guidance, by Doreen Virtue, (c. 1998), p. 220

Afterword

My hope is that you will find something that you can take for yourself from this work. The Holy Spirit is working with each of us in a unique way. I think that organized religion has a role, but we shouldn't get stuck there. Our destiny is to rise above and through what religion has to offer.

We have all placed ourselves in the best environment to accomplish our soul's goals for this lifetime. For me, one of my life lessons is to not let different political persuasions or people with different opinions get me down, angry and upset. The current political climate (CE 2017) is fertile ground for learning that lesson. Where anger and violence seem to be the new normal, I am challenged to work harder to find an inner peace in all that. I try to send love to the leaders of our country and drift off to sleep by envisioning a world at peace and how that feels, sending the world thoughts of peace. I believe that our thoughts reach beyond us and have an influence.

I am grateful every day for the gift of life, for my wife and the life we have, for the wisdom we have sought and received, for having very few regrets in my life and for any challenges life presents to me. Challenges can be a health issue, a relationship or financial issue, etc.

I do not want to be seen as "religious" but rather as an integral person who projects love and kindness by just being who I am. God is Love and I want only to be the face of love to others in how I touch their lives. In that way, we participate in the act of creation. Love is all about creation. Perhaps that is why I shun belonging to any faith-based group. I don't need that any more. I see and now firmly believe that the One I owe my very existence to loves me unconditionally. There is no fear whatsoever in that realization – but a genuine joy. I don't worry about anything but see all events in life as an opportunity to learn something and it was likely something that I planned to happen before I was born. Life doesn't have to be scary.

Death doesn't have to be scary either. I believe that life on earth is the worst it gets for us. I don't believe in a hell in the afterlife. When we die, we leave this world behind. That will be the happiest day of our lives, because we finally get to leave it all behind.

I love my life! I didn't realize it could be this joyful and peaceful in my 70's. That is what this book is about, a testimonial that you too can have a life that well before you reach my age; it just took me that long. A *Course in Miracles* says:

> *Vision is freely given to those who ask to see. The Holy Spirit, will of himself, fill every mind that so makes room for Him. Leave room for Him, and you will find yourself so filled with power that nothing will prevail against your peace. And this will be the test by which you recognize that you have understood.* [1]

Believe it! This book is a snapshot of a work-in-progress. It reflects some insights at this point in time.

Each of us is on a quest to evolve to greater awareness and a greater ability to love. The more we can act out of love versus fear, the happier we will be. Our Creator wants us to be happy - not sad, hopeful – not despairing, joyful – not depressed, spiritually alive – and not asleep. Our loving Father wants only what is best for us.

It is my hope that this will also serve to help my friends and family members to better understand my interest in the spiritual aspects of life long after I'm gone.

May you ask and work with your guides for a more vibrant spiritual awareness. The spirit world is eager to assist us in finding our truth in navigating this world of illusions. Congratulations on having the perseverance to read through these pages. May the Holy Spirit bless you with vision, insight and joy as you live out your days.

---

[1] A Course in Miracles, (c. 1977), Text 14 XI:15.5

Personal Creed by the author:

I believe that God's love is without conditions and that Jesus came to bring us that message.
That He became man and lived among us and is our brother.
I believe that all people are cherished children of the Father and my brothers and sisters together with Jesus are the Sonship of our Father.
I believe I am precious in God's eyes and there is nothing I can do that will keep God's love from me.
I believe He has given me the treasured gift of free will and will never interfere with my freedom to choose.
I believe that what I experience is the result of the choices I make and what I decide to see.
I believe that the Holy Spirit is God's presence in the world and that His guidance and help are available to me if I but ask.
I believe that God lives in each of us: we are created in His image and likeness and God's will for me is also my will and what He wants for me is only for my own good.
I believe that we are called to forgive others and ourselves.
I ask to be guided along a path that is best for me and will bring me inner peace, and ask for the wisdom
and the vision to see through the illusions of this world and to help others along their spiritual paths.
I look forward to coming Home to be with Our Father, at one with the Sonship at the end of this lifetime singing a song of eternal gratitude for His unfailing love.

Acknowledgements

This book is the result of many sets of hands. From the beginning, my wife, Barbara, has been a good sounding board and editor. She is my long time love, friend and partner in this work and world. Her name should be on the cover too. Her fingerprints are also on this book. She has been very helpful in reviewing every chapter and verse for grammar and spelling, not to mention the time that this all has taken to complete and her patience with it all. I didn't realize how much time it would take to bring it to this form.

Several close friends have reviewed chapters and encouraged me to persevere and push on to finish this work. At the risk of leaving someone out, I will not list the names here, but you know who you are and my heartfelt thanks for the gift of your ideas.

To those who first read the unpolished text and gave me good feedback, I am grateful. That you took the time to read all of it is a significant time commitment as well as providing valued insights.

To my editor, Tina Rosekrans of Edit This One Inc., who took this text and helped to bring it to its published form. Thanks for your patience plowing through this first kind of a book for you. It takes a variety of skills to produce a book. I greatly appreciate what you do.

I recognize the contributions of my spirit guides and angels who gave me thoughts I did not think and the inspiration they provided that is included in these pages.

To several authors of the new spirituality, I am grateful.

I value the insights of John Shelby Spong for his Biblical and Jesus scholarship and putting the Bible in perspective for me. Without a valid critique of this sacred text, I would not have come to the conclusions you find in this work.

Philip Gulley and John Mulholland have published books that demonstrate to me that they are thinking about what they do and why they do anything. Their insights on implementing the Gospel message are beacons for those with questions about the Christian practice. They are living life's questions - a reflective Christianity.

Steve Rother with *Lightworkers.com* has provided insights on the psychology of the soul; what we are about, why we are here and what our souls need and want. He teaches what nourishes the soul and what doesn't.

Gregg Braden has authored several books, which were beneficial in writing the chapter on prayer. His research on ancient wisdom is needed today. His work is insightful and respected.

To the Foundation for Inner Peace and the work they have done to bring *A Course in Miracles* to us all, my undying gratitude. Barbara and I have studied this sacred text for more than ten years now and it has opened our eyes to the greater reality of the life of spirit. It enabled the vision we live by today.

Thanks to Mari Perron who scribed *A Course of Love*, a companion book to *A Course in Miracles*. This teaches us to live with mind and heart working together to love with genuine compassion.

Other authors, who helped me formulate the vision presented in this book, include Anita Moorjani, Wayne Dyer, Ram Dass, Desmond Tutu, Marianne Williamson, Robert Holden, Neale Donald Walsch, James Kavanaugh, Gary Zukav, Miguel Ruiz, Doreen Virtue, Mitch Albom and Cheryl Richardson. I recommend any and all of the above. All of these are visionaries for our time and the road that lies ahead.

I am open to hearing from readers. Let's talk. I have an email set up for this purpose – btlindsley41@gmail.com

Appendix

Recommended Readings and Resources

Chapter 1
A Return to Love, by Marianne Williamson, (c. 1992) This was one of her first works on *A Course in Miracles*.
The Unmistakable Touch of Grace, by Cheryl Richardson, (c. 2005) Cheryl is a life coach.
Conversations with God-1, by Neale Donald Walsch, (c. 1995) Neale is a spiritual teacher for modern times and has authored many books.
Shift Happens, by Robert Holden, (c. 2011) Short readings & reflections based on the *A Course in Miracles*.
Dying to be Me, by Anita Moorjani, (c. 2012) Insights from her near death experience.

Chapter 2
If God is Love, by Philip Gulley and James Mulholland, (c. 2004) These are two pastors who live a reflective Christianity.
The Holy Bible, Luke 15:11ff The Prodigal Son.
The Misunderstood God, by Darin Hufford (c. 2009).
The Sins of Scripture, by John Shelby Spong, (c. 2005) The latest Biblical scholarship. He is also a Jesus scholar and has authored many books on these subjects.

Chapter 3
A Return to Love, by Marianne Williamson, (c. 1992).
Dying To Be Me, by Anita Moorjani, (c. 2012).
Home With God - In a life that never ends, by Neal Donald Walsch (c. 2005).
If God Is Love, by Philip Gulley and James Mulholland, (c. 2004).

Chapter 4
Change your Thoughts – Change your Mind, by Wayne Dyer, (c. 2007) Short meditations on each verse of the Tao Te Ching.
The Sins of Scripture, by Bishop John Shelby Spong, (c. 2006).
A Course in Miracles, Scribed by Helen Schucman, (c. 1976).
A Course of Love, Scribed by Mari Perron, (c. 2014), a companion work to A Course in Miracles.
The Tao Te Ching by Lau Tzu, Authored @500 BCE.
Shift Happens, by Robert Holden (c. 2011) Short meditations themed on a spirituality for our time.
The Qu'ran or Koran, authored @650 CE.
Dying To Be Me: My Journey from Cancer, to Near Death, to True Healing, by Anita Moorjani, (c. 2012).

Chapter 5
The Seat of the Soul, by Gary Zukav, (c. 1989) A very readable description about the soul's journey.
Shift Happens, by Robert Holden, (c. 2011).
The New Revelation, by Neale Donald Walsch (c. 2002).
Healing the Soul of America, by Marianne Williamson, (c. 1997).

God Has A Dream, by Desmond Tutu, (c. 2004).

Chapter 6
Spiritual Psychology by Steve Rother, (c. 2004), A seminal work on this subject.
Steve Rother's website: https://www.Espavo.org
Welcome Home, by Steve Rother, (c. 2002).
If Grace is True-God Will Save Every Person, by Philip Gulley (c. 2003), a book on universal salvation.
Five People You Meet In Heaven, by Mitch Albom, (c. 2006) An example of what a life review is about.
The Seat of the Soul, by Gary Zukav, (c. 1989).
Dying To Be Me: My Journey from Cancer, to Near Death, to True Healing, by Anita Moorjani, (c. 2012).
The New Revelation, by Neale Donald Walsch, (c. 2002).

Chapter 7
God Lives, by James Kavanaugh, (c. 1993) A Jesuit priest who left the Catholic Church.
The Evolution of Faith, by Philip Gulley, (c. 2011).
Why Christianity Must Change or Die, by John Shelby Spong, (c. 1998), a critical analysis of modern day organized religion.
Conversations With God-2, by Neale Donald Walsch, (c. 1997).
Occupy Spirituality, by Adam Bucko and Matthew Fox, (c. 2013) These are two questioning and reflective writers.
The Sins of Scripture, by John Shelby Spong, (c. 2005).

Chapter 8
Secrets of the Lost Mode of Prayer, by Gregg Braden, (c. 2006) Gregg has done extensive research into ancient wisdom which has been lost to our time. He has authored many books on the new spirituality.
The Divine Matrix, by Gregg Braden, (c. 2008).
Conversations with God-2, by Neale Donald Walsch, (c. 1997).
The Law of Attraction: The Basics of the Teachings of Abraham, by Esther and Jerry Hicks (c. 2006) Two spiritual teachers who channel spirit guides.

Chapter 9
Soul to Soul, by Gary Zukav, (c. 2011).
Pretending to be Human, by Steve Rother, (c. 2013), the human experience in the context of soul history.
Dying Well, by Dr. Ira Byock, (c. 1997) Ira has written several books on death and the dying process.
How We Die, by Sherwin Nuland, (c. 1995) A detailed account of the changes in our bodies as we die.
Dying to Be Me, by Anita Moorjani, (c. 2012).
The Storm Before The Calm, by Neale Donald Walsch, (c. 2011) A book about new spiritual understandings.

Websites:
End of Life University (EOLU), www.eoluniversity.com
This website is helpful in understanding and
managing the dying process. Dr. Karen Wyatt is founder.

Chapter 10
Eternal Life: A New Vision, by John Shelby Spong, (c. 2009).
The Four Agreements, by Miguel Ruiz, (c. 1997), the Toltec wisdom. Very practical.
The Fifth Agreement, by Miguel Ruiz, (c. 2010).
The Unmistakable Touch of Grace, by Cheryl Richardson, (c. 2005).

How to recognize and respond to the spiritual guideposts in your life:
The Seeker's Guide, by Elizabeth Lesser, (c. 1999) She writes for the spiritual seeker.

Websites:
www.ProgressiveChristianity.org – a forum for leading thinkers and writers working with Christian reformation.
www.cwg.org – Neale Donald Walsch website. Neale is a prolific spiritual author.
www.drwaynedyer.com – Wayne Dyer many books on spirituality and personal growth.
www.eckharttolle.com – Eckhart Tolle is a leading spiritual thinker.
www.johnshelbyspong.com – Spong is a good source for current biblical scholarship. He is also a Jesus scholar – very good material.
www.greggbraden.com – insightful writings applying the treasures of ancient wisdom to today's world.
www.deepakchopra.com – author of many books.
www.cherylrichardson.com – Cheryl is a life coach and author.

www.acim.org – the official website for ***A Course in Miracles.***
www.acourseoflove.org – Mari Perron's website for ***A Course of Love.***
www.marianne.com – Home page for Marianne Williamson.
www.seatofthesoul.com – Gary Zukav website.
www.caringbridge.org – website for people suffering from disease and injury.
www.posthope.org – website for people suffering from disease.

www.ingramcontent.com/pod-product-compliance
Lightning Source LLC
Chambersburg PA
CBHW020000050426
42450CB00005B/266